What Your Dog is Thinking

What Your Dog is Thinking

Everything you need to know to understand your pet

BO SÖDERSTRÖM

First published in Sweden in 2017 by Bonnier Fakta as *Hur tänker din hund?*
This edition published in 2019 by John Murray Learning, an imprint of Hodder & Stoughton. An Hachette UK Company.

Translation by Daniel Lind

A CIP catalogue record for this title is available from the British Library.

Paperback ISBN 978 1 473 68836 0
eBook ISBN 978 1 473 68838 4

1

Typeset by Cenveo® Publisher Services.

Printed and bound in Great Britain by Clays Ltd, Elcograf S.p.A.

John Murray Learning policy is to use papers that are natural, renewable and recyclable products and made from wood grown in sustainable forests. The logging and manufacturing processes are expected to conform to the environmental regulations of the country of origin.

Contents

Preface

THE BOOK YOU are holding in your hand brings together the results of recent research into dog behaviour. More scientific articles on the subject are being published than ever before – about one new one a day, 365 days a year – but it's not very often that these interesting studies reach the general reader.

What Your Dog is Thinking contains the latest scientific findings relating to dog training and the relationship between dogs and people. It is my hope that reading this book will help you understand your dog a bit better. At the end of each section you'll find a quick bulleted summary of the most important findings.

I hope you'll find reading this book fun as well as educational, just as it has been for me while writing it. It has been my aim to write in a way that is interesting but not too personal. I really hope you enjoy reading about man's best friend!

Bo Söderström

Introduction

WE'RE MORE ENGAGED with our dogs than ever before. Our dogs attend daycare, eat with us, and sleep in our beds. And it's as natural for us to take our dogs to the vet as to take our children to the doctor. In other words, we do our best to ensure that our dogs feel as good as is physically possible. At the same time, we also try to understand what is going on inside our dog's mind: we wonder what our dog really thinks and how we can understand it better.

In recent decades we have undoubtedly changed our view of dogs. Just as in children's education, today's learning models for dogs are mainly based on so-called positive reinforcement of good behaviour. The dog training trade has been professionalized and many training methods today have their basis in science. For example, in Sweden during the 1970s the Swedish Working

Dog Association was an overwhelmingly male organization that worked in tracking, searching, retrieving and protection. Today, by contrast, it's an organization dominated by women who run dog sports such as obedience classes, agility courses and freestyle.

The majority of today's training methods are based more on enjoyment and fellowship with our dogs than on hierarchies and dominance. Research by the Swedish Central Bureau of Statistics from 2012 shows that dog ownership is on the rise in my country.

Yet Sweden – where dog ownership is most common in households without children – is far behind other nations when it comes to the adoption of dogs as man's best friend.

Whilst the number of dogs has increased steadily in my country, a smaller proportion of households in Sweden have dogs compared to the other Nordic countries. And if we look outside Scandinavia, there are just two countries in Europe – Austria and Switzerland – with a smaller proportion of household dogs.

In Eastern Europe, a much larger proportion of countries have dogs – the pattern is only broken by Russia, a nation that prizes the cat, a far more common pet in the region.

All told, there 900 million dogs in the world, yet before we explore dog ownership more fully, we must remember that more than 700 million live as village or street dogs. Many of these dogs may be loosely connected to one or more households, but they roam the streets of villages and cities, living off rubbish and handouts.

The situation couldn't be more different in the UK, where the dog is regarded as a family member!

In this book you will read the results of the latest research into 'man's best friend' and increase and enrich your understanding

PERCENTAGE OF HOUSEHOLDS WITH A DOG IN EUROPEAN COUNTRIES

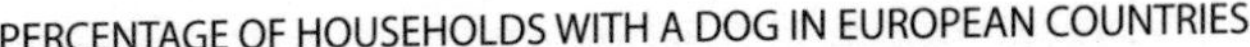

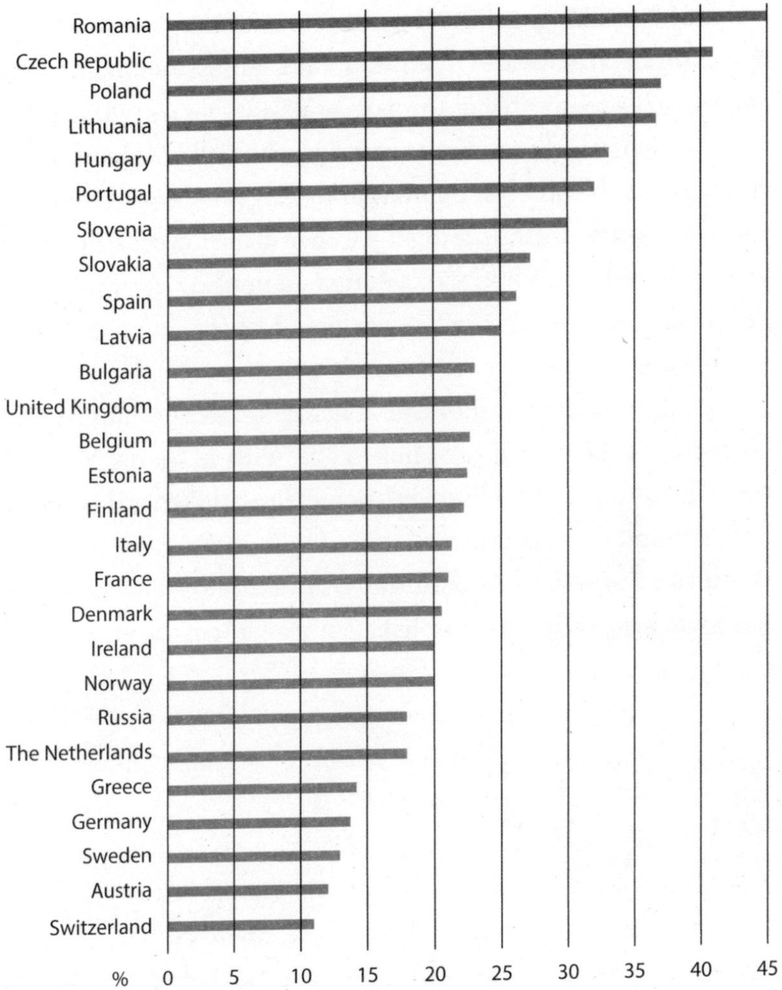

The diagram shows the percentage of households in European countries that have a dog. In total, there are about 75 million dogs in Europe. Source: The European Pet Food Industry 2012

of your relationship with your dog. The research has often focused on looking at how dogs and people interact, in a bond that is often so close and intense that it's impossible to interpret a dog's behaviour without the presence of its owner.

By asking questions about your dog, you will also learn more about how to resolve the issues that you, as a dog owner, may encounter – without compromising either your dog's wellbeing or your own peace of mind. For example, if your dog is aggressive, fearful or anxious, you will learn how to help your pet – and what actions to avoid.

The book also describes the fascinating history and origins of dogs and how they adapted to life with humans. You will discover when and how humans domesticated the wolf and how the wolf and the dog differ.

All this knowledge is built on recent cutting-edge research – based on articles mainly published since January 2015.

The science behind this book

The language has been enriched with two new phrases in recent years: 'fact resistance' and 'filter bubble'. According to *Language Magazine*, fact resistance is a situation where one isn't affected by facts that oppose one's own perception, while a filter bubble is created when Internet giants such as Facebook customize what the individual experiences on the Internet, so that opinions opposing our own aren't shown in our feed.

Fact resistance and filter bubbles together create an environment where emotions prevail over reason. It's as far from the scientific method as one can go. But why should we put our trust in science?

In my opinion, the biggest advantage with the scientific method is that scientists openly show, without restrictions, how they come to their conclusions. Scientific articles have a specific structure called IMRaD – Introduction, Methods, Results and

Discussion. It might seem rigid, but this structure is crucial for researchers to be able to quickly search for information and form an opinion about the quality of a piece of research. The authors of a scientific article indicate in their introduction what's been written before on the subject, and how their study builds on already-established knowledge.

In other words, it's the opposite of a filter bubble. In the scientific method, scientists describe the process they undertook to answer the question they asked in their introduction. The methods used are described so precisely that other scientists can repeat a given study and receive approximately the same result.

I say 'approximately' because the science used in this book is unfortunately seldom exact; in ethology, scientists study animal behaviour, and in ecology they study the interaction between living organisms and the environment they live in. All animals are individuals and react differently when exposed to the same stimuli. It would be strange if that weren't the case. Out of regard for individual variations, researchers therefore study many different animals in as controlled a way as possible. In practice, this means scientists right from the beginning try to rule out as many sources of error as they can – that is, factors that could affect the animals but that aren't interesting for that particular study.

Most of the studies described in this book have used controlled experiments. In other words, the researchers have randomly divided dogs into a trial group and a control group. They have made the circumstances between the two groups as equal as possible, apart from the factor they want to test.

They have then systematically described behaviours or measured something using the two groups. The results from the two groups are later compared with the help of statistics. That is why a larger dog sample in each group is required, because otherwise the occasional dog with odd behaviours could give an incorrect view of the group as a whole. The scientists conclude by putting their own results into a larger context, showing openly whether or not others have drawn the same conclusions. They also talk about the strengths and weaknesses of their study and how to improve it in the future.

To further ensure that researchers are neither fact resistant nor living in a filter bubble, more checks are made before the results are published in a science journal. All articles go through a scientific, or peer, review, performed partly by the journal editors and partly by other scientists in the same field. Every detail is scrutinized, and sometimes the researchers are required to perform further experiments and analysis. It's more common than not that they have to rewrite the text twice or even three times before inspectors and editors are satisfied and the article can be published. But nothing written in a scientific article is ever the final truth; it is always a work in progress. We can only claim adequate scientific support (evidence) for a conclusion once enough articles have been published showing the same thing.

This book reflects the fact that researching dog behaviour has become more and more popular. I searched through the *Web of Knowledge*, the world's largest article database for scientific literature, with the search words *dog* in combination with *behaviour* or *behavior* (British or American English spelling). In the 1980s fewer than 150 articles were published, in the 1990s more than 300 articles, in the 2000s more than 1,000 articles, and between 2010 and 2016 almost 1,500 articles. In other words, the number of scientific articles about dogs has more than doubled each decade.

The Swedish researcher in ethology Per Jensen has written several books summarizing contemporary research into dog behaviour. In his book *Dogs That Feel Shame – Myth or Reality?* (2014), Jensen writes: 'As I'm putting the final touches to the text, I discover new interesting research papers, published in the past few days, that I should have included in the book.' It's just like that! Research work into pet animal behaviour has surged since 2010 and new knowledge is added every day, with questions developed from earlier studies.

To reduce the risk of overlap with earlier books, in this book I've chosen to summarize the most interesting articles published between 1 January 2015 and 1 May 2016. One might think it's a tight selection – but it isn't: from the database I downloaded and read the abstracts (summaries) of 330 articles published during that period. The abstracts gave a good idea of the content, so I used that information to select the most interesting articles. My focus was to pick articles that tickled my curiosity.

I don't claim that this book will cover all aspects of dog behaviour, but it was the access to interesting scientific articles that was decisive. You as a reader don't have to worry, however, that you'll miss out on exciting results just because I've restricted the selection. I've also included especially interesting articles that were published before 2015. I found out about these articles mainly because they were mentioned in the later articles I read. In total, I have summarized the results and conclusions of more than 150 articles for this book.

These articles can be sorted into seven areas, which form the chapters of this book: 'The sociable dog', 'The interaction between dog and human', 'Good contact with your dog', 'Problem solving', 'Your dog's health', 'Your dog's senses' and 'How dogs originated'. In every chapter I've made three or four further subdivisions.

The research articles themselves obviously offer much more information and detail than I can mention. You may not find everything equally interesting, but if you want to know more about any aspect of dog behaviour, you can find the relevant article listed in the reference section at the back of the book. I indicate there, chapter by chapter, who has written what.

Research is teamwork and the author list for articles becomes longer with every year that passes. Sometimes it could be misleading only to refer to the first author when it's perhaps the last one who's done all the hard work. Unfortunately, it's not possible for me to make that distinction. I always refer to the first author.

How does it work then when you're searching for a specific article? Look up the webpage dx.doi.org and type in exactly what comes after 'doi' in the reference list. That will take you automatically to the correct article. These articles are increasingly becoming free to download as PDF or directly to your screen.

1

The sociable dog

DOGS ARE SOCIABLE creatures that love being in the company of others. But while there may be many advantages to living in a group – you can, for example, always find a playmate – there are also disadvantages. How do dogs solve conflicts within the group? And how should we interpret the ritualized signals that dogs use to communicate their status? This chapter explains the importance of socializing your puppy and how you can test its personality, as well as explaining the significance of dog play and the role of hierarchy and dominance within the dog's social group.

Your puppy's social development

The dog's ability to communicate with us humans is unique. During the 13,000 years that we've lived together, humans have been able to gradually refine the dog's behaviour and social competence through breeding. But research shows that hereditary factors aren't enough to explain whether or not a particular dog will be friendly, affectionate and obedient as an adult. We must also actively engage with and raise the puppy in a secure environment for it to become stable and agreeable as an adult – it must be socialized.

Research into dog behaviour has stressed the importance of socializing a puppy at a young age. Otherwise there's a risk that the adult dog may develop behavioural problems. The puppy stage has three phases that are especially significant for the dog's social development.

The first phase happens from birth to about three weeks, when the mother plays a determining role. Sight and hearing gradually develop during this period, but above all else the puppy is dependent on the sense of touch to explore and experience its surroundings.

Not all dogs' mothers are engaged with their puppies and this can have consequences for a puppy's temperament later in life. The Swedish researchers Pernilla Foyer, Erik Wilsson and Per Jensen showed this in an experiment published in 2016. The researchers wanted to investigate why only one out of three German Shepherds within the military's breeding programme had a temperament that corresponded to the set requirements of service dogs.

Could it be connected to German Shepherd mothers being worse at touching their puppies during the early stages? To answer that question, scientists followed 22 new German Shepherd mothers and their puppies during their three first weeks of life. They recorded through surveillance cameras

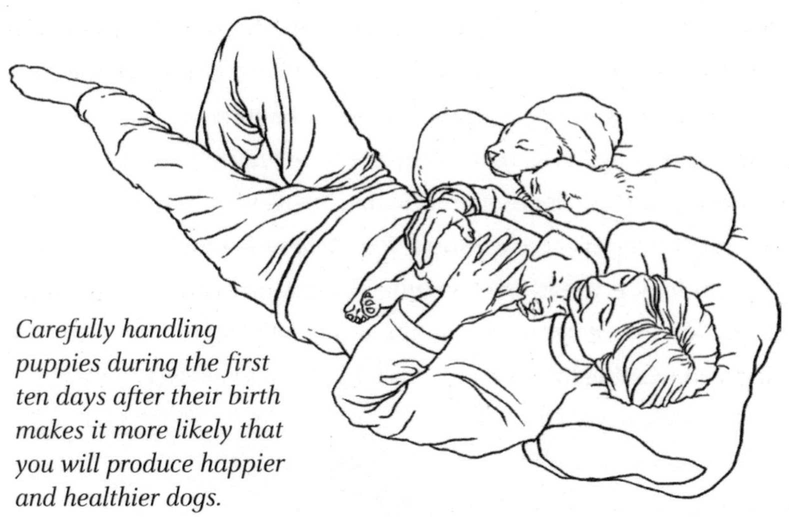

Carefully handling puppies during the first ten days after their birth makes it more likely that you will produce happier and healthier dogs.

when the mother suckled, licked, smelled or rested in direct contact with her puppies.

They recorded the mothers' behaviours at four different times – at one, seven, 14 and 21 days after birth – every other hour during that day. The surveillance camera showed that there were consistent differences in how much the mothers interacted with the puppies. The scientists therefore divided the mothers into two groups: one that touched their puppies frequently and another that did it more seldom. They later compared how the puppies' temperament had developed at a revisit 15 to 20 months later.

The scientists found a clear connection: the now-adult German Shepherds that had had more engaged mothers during their puppyhood were more sociable with humans and more curious, exploring new objects to a greater degree. It seems that the mother's level of engagement with her puppies influences her puppies' temperament as adults. This research shows why the military, when considering dogs in the future, should consider the level of engagement of the dogs' mothers.

Breeders can also help mothers to socialize with their pups by handling the puppies carefully during the first ten days after birth. Several studies show that this may contribute to more secure, less anxious and even healthier adult dogs. In an article published in *Veterinary Medicine*, Tiffani Howell and her colleagues emphasize that this could be particularly important at professional kennels, where the puppies don't get as much attention as they would do with a private breeder. Because touch is the most important sense during the puppy's first three weeks, its siblings also contribute to early emotional experiences. If the puppy has no siblings, the breeder should give it more loving attention to support its social development.

Siblings are also very important in the second key phase of social development, which is from three to about 12 weeks. After about three weeks, the puppies no longer need constant supervision from their mother and start to play with each other instead. At about five weeks old, the puppies become more alert to their surroundings and they can become frightened by sudden sounds, foreign environments and people. The start of this period varies according to breed, as Mary Morrow and her colleagues showed in an article published in the *Journal of Veterinary Behavior* in 2015.

In time, when the puppies have learned what is dangerous and what is not, their fear subsides. During this phase it's important that the puppies have the opportunity to be with many different humans. Research shows that puppies that haven't been exposed to people before the age of 14 weeks may develop a problematic relationship with humans later in life.

Socializing with various humans and experiencing new surroundings are especially important when the puppies are between three and 12 weeks old. But for a good long-term relationship, people should continue to socialize with the puppies during the third phase, which commences from the age of 12 weeks and lasts until they're sexually mature. This is when the puppies will be able to carefully try out all the joys and dangers that adult dogs could face: other dogs, other pets such as cats and horses, wild animals, unfamiliar children, adult humans and more. By socializing the puppy, you get a confident dog that doesn't feel needlessly scared or aggressive in new and unfamiliar situations.

Not to socialize a dog might have obvious negative consequences, but the key issue is: how much socializing is enough? Is there a risk that we overdo it with our good intentions? If we subject a dog to too many courses and too much stimuli, do we risk causing confusion instead of creating a sense of security? A wide range of courses are available for puppies and new dog owners, and many research teams have studied whether and how these might affect an adult dog's behaviour.

A review article by Tiffani Howell and her colleagues shows that there is no strong support in science for the benefits of puppy courses. A puppy that grows up in a typical home is exposed daily to different stimuli and experiences that prepare them for adulthood. This is probably enough to socialize the puppy. Controlled experiments are unfortunately rare, and it's next to impossible to determine whether the adult dog's behaviour is a consequence of a puppy course or of the variety of other experiences the dog has had in its life. Therefore it's advisable to take the results of the studies with a pinch of salt.

The biggest benefit of a puppy course is perhaps for the humans, specifically those who have become dog owners for the first time. The course gives them an opportunity to meet other owners and exchange knowledge, and at the same time learn more about their dog's behaviour and how to deal with different situations.

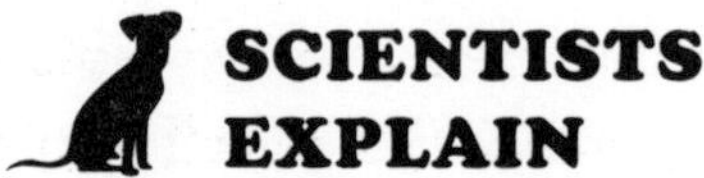

Your puppy's social development

- A puppy must be socialized in order to feel secure and become friendly as an adult.
- There are three key phases in a puppy's social development: 0–3 weeks, when touch is the most important sense; 3–12 weeks, when the puppy increasingly discovers its surroundings; and from 12 weeks until sexual maturity, when it discovers all the joys and dangers the adult dog might encounter, indoors and outdoors.

- The breeder and eventually the dog owner have an important role in socializing the puppy, by handling it and gradually introducing new stimuli.
- Puppy courses don't have a documented effect on an adult dog's behaviour, but they can be useful for new owners to exchange experiences.
- Studies show that puppies that haven't been exposed to humans before the age of 14 weeks risk developing a problematic relationship with humans later in life.

Personality tests

It's becoming increasingly popular for dog owners to test their puppy's personality. For puppies being trained to become service or assistance dogs, such tests could separate the wheat from the chaff early and help trainers decide which puppies are most appropriate for future training and deployment. A personality test may help you understand better your puppy's temperament and make it easier to know how to train your pet to overcome fears or other unwanted behaviours, as well as strengthen the puppy's positive attributes. Finally, a personality test can be a fun thing – now you can show everyone in black and white that your puppy really is as loveable and sociable as you think!

There are numerous ways to test a puppy's personality and it can sometimes be difficult to get to grips with the mass of personality tests published in the scientific literature and in handbooks aimed at the dog owner. Two articles published in 2015 could help you along the way.

The first is an overview article by Monica McGarrity and colleagues from the USA, where the researchers let experts determine which personality tests are the best. It's consumer advice à la *Which?*, but this time it's dog expert behavioural scientists who do the assessment. The first challenge for McGarrity and her colleagues was to choose a few abilities that still gave a complete image of the puppy's personality. Some researchers have claimed that as few as three abilities are needed, whereas others say as many as 11 are required.

From the published overview articles and models, McGarrity and her colleagues came up with nine abilities that needed to be assessed in order to gain a complete image of the personality. These were: 'social', 'frightened/nervous', 'active', 'exploring', 'bold/self-assured', 'reactive', 'aggressive', 'submissive' and 'willing to train'. You can see the most common adjectives to describe these attributes in the chart below.

After that, the researchers went through several large article databases that describe the results of various personality tests on puppies. They found 49 different publications containing 181 tests. Some of these tests were assessed as unreliable because they measured several of the nine attributes simultaneously. These were subsequently removed, which left 100.

Six experienced behavioural scientists with different backgrounds – but all experienced with dogs – quality-assured the

100 tests to determine whether each test was a good way to assess the attribute being tested. McGarrity and her colleagues determined it to be a consensus when four out of the six experts, irrespective of each other, had the same opinion. I'm describing this procedure in detail to show that the researchers took the consumer advice seriously. The results were discouraging, however: few of the tested puppies were exposed to a good measurement of the attributes being tested. Luckily, the experts managed to agree on at least one test per ability that worked well. See the chart below.

Nine attributes that together describe a puppy's personality

ATTRIBUTE	THE PUPPY IS …	EXPERTS' ADVICE ON 'THE BEST TEST'
Sociable	Loveable, extrovert, playful	An unknown person tries to play with the puppy.
Frightened and nervous	Generally nervous, shies away, timid, careful, cautious, sensitive	A new object is presented to the puppy. The researchers measure behaviours such as squatting, shivering, avoidance, etc.
Active	Physically active/ inactive, energetic, hyperactive, restless	The puppy is placed in a room with a chequered pattern on the floor. The researchers measure how far the puppy moves in a certain time.

Exploring	Curious, loves new things/challenges (behaviour to a new situation)	The puppy is placed in a room with unknown objects, such as large balls, a vacuum cleaner or new toys. The researchers measure the number of times the puppy approaches the objects.
Bold and self-assured	Determined, persistent, independent, opportunistic	The puppy negotiates an obstacle, like a stair. The researchers measure the puppy's speed and whether or not it hesitates.
Reactive	Excitable, has behaviour problems	The puppy goes out for a walk and receives surprises, e.g. a person unfolding an umbrella, or a live snake. The researchers measure how often and how strongly the puppy reacts.
Aggressive	Angry, bites, hostile	A person removes the food bowl from an eating puppy. The researchers measure the tail's and ears' position, growls, etc.

Submissive	Submissive, dominant	Siblings are placed in pairs with a chewing bone inside a pen. The researchers measure how long before the puppy shares the bone or if it keeps it to itself.
Willing to train	Obedient, distracted, cooperative, loyal, intelligent, attentive, sensible	A ball is thrown to the puppy. The researchers measure how often the puppy chases and returns the ball to the thrower, or if it becomes distracted by other people in the vicinity.

In the second article Lina Roth and Per Jensen investigated whether it's possible to conduct personality tests in a real-world setting. Most personality tests are conducted in specially adapted rooms without the owner present. This is unfortunate because it's the relationship between the dog and its owner that's the most interesting. That's where it needs to work every day. To study whether it was possible to assess a dog's personality in a more everyday environment, Roth and Jensen looked up different training courses for dogs outside Vimmerby and Linköping in Sweden.

They studied 85 dogs that were undertaking training – puppy course, obedience course, freestyle, agility or tracking course – together with their owners. The dogs were filmed at a distance, as the owner stood with their dog on a lead behind a plastic cone with kitchen roll painted in black and white attached to the top of it. The dog owner was asked to fill out a form where he or she answered questions about the dog's personality.

In the meantime, the dog was free (while on a lead) to act without a command from its owner. The leader approached on three occasions: to hand out the survey, to give a pen, and then to collect the survey. The procedure was filmed for three minutes, and by studying the films Roth and Jensen could assess the dogs' reactions to the new object (the cone with kitchen roll), the stranger (the test leader), the owner and the other dogs waiting on the side. After the first filming sequence, the dog owners walked around several cones in a wide circle as they were filmed for another 30 seconds. The researchers registered and categorized how often the dog reacted to the object (the cone), the stranger (the test leader), its owner and the other dogs during this short time.

The researchers found that the dogs executed 22 different behaviours, for example 'look towards', 'smell', 'pull lead' and so on. They were able to put all the behaviours together with the help of advanced statistics: 'sociable', 'exploring', 'curious/still', 'seeking contact' and 'restless'. After that they compared the results with how the owners had described the dogs in the survey. The results corresponded surprisingly well.

If the owner had described their dog as sociable, it showed similar characteristics in this behavioural study. Roth and Jensen also found that the dogs on the training course's second day were more focused on the owners and less on the environment than on the first day. They could also conclude that young dogs were more sociable and curious than older dogs in general, and that female dogs looked for more physical contact with their owners than male dogs. Both of these results correspond with earlier behavioural studies.

This seemingly simple method of describing dogs' personality in a quite everyday environment for the dogs was very effective. As a bonus, it was also possible to document how the dogs interacted with their owner and with other dogs.

In the increasing number of articles published in scientific journals evaluating different ways to measure dogs' personality, there was confusion about concepts for a long time. The same attribute meant different things to different researchers, and a large number of tests showed things they weren't supposed to show. That is why Monica McGarrity and her colleagues have helped researchers as well as practitioners to produce a list of simple tests containing the most essential attributes that comprise a puppy's personality.

Lina Roth and Per Jensen also show that tests can be done more easily and closer to reality without losing authenticity. Personality tests are very likely to become more precise in the future.

Personality tests

- Of the large number of available personality tests, few measure the intended attribute in a perfect way.
- A complete description of a puppy's personality comprises the attributes 'sociable', 'frightened/nervous', 'active', 'exploring', 'bold/self-assured', 'reactive', 'aggressive', 'submissive', and 'willing to train'.
- Researchers have gone through published articles on personality tests and produced a list of simple tests of these attributes (as shown in the table earlier in the chapter).
- Personality tests without the owner present aren't very true to life and can be misleading.
- If you are interested in personality testing your puppy, there are many locally available – try contacting your national Kennel Club.

Dog play

It's difficult to miss the exuberance radiated by a playful dog. Researchers have found the significance of dog play hard to describe and understand in words. Do dogs that play a great deal have more advantages than dogs that play less? And how is it that even adult dogs play to a large degree? For thousands of years, humans have preferred to breed dogs that show juvenile traits such as playfulness – not just because dogs that play often awaken positive emotions in humans, but also because playful dogs are easier to train than aggressive ones.

It's also not entirely unthinkable that the degree of playfulness in wolves was a decisive factor for which individuals were bred. The first agriculturists probably preferred the wolves that weren't just less afraid of humans but also relaxed enough to play with them. Playful wolves probably learned more and could therefore be more easily trained to perform simple tasks for humans. We obviously don't know if this is what happened, but it's an appealing idea that could explain why many adult dogs today are interested in playing. But why do dogs play? What do they get out of playing?

We get many of the answers in a very readable summary article published in the journal *Behavioural Processes* (2014). In the article the researcher John Bradshaw and colleagues differentiate between three different types of play: dogs that play with an object alone; dogs that play with other dogs; and dogs that play with people. Easiest to explain from an adaptive perspective – that is, the long-term advantage to the dog – is the playing with people.

Play strengthens the bond between dog and owner, and many studies show that it also decreases levels of the stress hormone cortisol in both dog and human, as the 'happiness hormones' – endorphin and oxytocin, among others – are released. Owners who punish less and play more with their dog also get a more obedient pet – a positive spiral emerges. But what advantages does the adult dog receive from playing with other dogs?

Bradshaw and his colleagues concluded that dogs who know each other well have set common play rules. Depending on who their playmate is, a certain dog tries to 'win' or 'lose' the play fights. This can be a way of confirming long-term relationships between dog friends. Play between dog and human seems to happen on more equal terms than that between dog and dog. A dog, for example, relinquishes a toy more easily to a human – to have the opportunity to continue the play – than to another dog. Various toys generally extend the play. Think of the happiness many dogs show when they time and again fetch a thrown stick or have a tug-of-war for a glove. Dogs play best in a social context and dog toys made for playing with alone are not as much fun. Even if dogs quickly tire of new toys, the ones that sound and move unpredictably seem to be the most attractive – in other words, toys that remind them most of prey animals. The incentive is then different from that of social play.

Dogs that live as pets have a secure and cosy life. They are therefore not exposed to the disadvantages that play can have for wild animals. It requires energy for a wild animal to play and this must be compensated for by an increased food intake. During play, wild animals aren't as attentive to their surroundings and the risk of an attack from a predator increases. Finally, there's also the risk that the animal injures itself during play. It would be interesting to study how much stray adult dogs play, but as yet no scientist has taken on that task.

Research has now revealed why dogs adopt this particular body position when they want to play.

It's not particularly far-fetched to assume that dogs which struggle to find food or partners don't play as much. Charles Darwin, 'the father of evolution', described the dog's play position in his book *The Expression of the Emotions in Man and Animals* in 1872. We all know about it: the dog stands directly turned towards another dog or human, with legs stretched along the ground and its bottom sticking up in the air. Its face is full of exuberance and it communicates loud and clear: 'Come and play with me!'

But how come the dog shows this stereotypical behaviour as a play signal? Does the body position have a function in actual play? It wasn't until 2016 – almost 150 years after the play position was described scientifically – that researchers tried to explain in detail the reason for this signal. In a 2016 article in the magazine *Behavioural Processes*, Sarah-Elizabeth Byosiere and her colleagues evaluated four different hypotheses for the dog's play position:

- **To resume play:** It's a ritualized signal to the receiver that the dog wants to resume play, if it's stopped.
- **To clarify good intentions:** It's a ritualized signal to clarify the dog's good intentions after having performed a behaviour that could easily be misinterpreted as aggressive, in this case playfully biting the play partner's head or neck and then directly shaking its own head from side to side.
- **To take a better strategic position:** It's the best physical position to be able to escape quickly or attack the partner in playful ways.
- **To synchronize behaviours:** The play partners are mirroring each other's behaviours to show that they're both willing to play, thereby developing or confirming a long-term relationship.

The best thing about these four hypotheses is that each one can be set up for testable predictions – that is, something that should happen if this particular hypothesis is true. During a period of ten years, researchers filmed interactions in pairs between 16 neutered pet dogs. They ended up evaluating over 400 different occasions when dogs took play positions, each one lasting two seconds on average. It turned out that the dogs played more, with fewer breaks, after one of the dogs had taken up the play position. In other words, the prediction supported the hypothesis about resuming play.

Exposing the abdomen during play doesn't have to be a sign of submission.

It also turned out that dogs mirror each other's play behaviours directly after one of them has taken the play position. The hypothesis about synchronizing behaviours got support in the results as well. None of the other hypotheses corresponded with the results, however. In an earlier article, the researchers found support for the hypothesis that the play position showed good intentions, but that could be because the researchers had included puppies in the study.

Playful stabs in the neck are much more common with young siblings than adult dogs. The researchers point out that the desire to play, and how intense the play becomes, varies depending on how well the dogs know each other. Sometimes the play position is followed by one of the dogs lying on its back with legs in the air, exposing the abdomen. In this context, the ritualized play signal would seem to be clear.

However, a recently published Master's dissertation by Kerri Norman from Canada shows that it's actually unusual for dogs to take the supine position as an invitation to play. The dogs only took the supine position after they'd been in the play position in 5 per cent of the cases. Once play had started, the supine position was used as part of a fighting technique – either with an offensive aim to make a lunge towards the playmate's throat or as a defensive aim to protect the neck against attacks. Norman couldn't conclude that the supine position showed submissiveness.

On the other hand, she pointed out that it's important to know about the dogs' relationship. It's more probable that it shows status if one of the dogs takes a supine position in a situation where they're not playing.

SCIENTISTS EXPLAIN

Dog play

- The dog's play position of outstretched front legs and bottom in the air is a ritualized signal to resume play after a temporary break.
- Playmates usually mirror each other's behaviours after a play position.
- A supine position during play is a form of fighting technique to make (playful) lunges or for self-defence.
- Play between dog and human decreases stress and releases happiness hormones in both.
- Play between dog and human is conducted on more equal terms than play between dogs.
- Dogs mostly play in social contexts. The most fun solo play for dogs includes objects that remind them of prey.
- Play entails a cost for wild animals, but the safe and well-nourished pet dog doesn't have to pay a price for playing.

Hierarchy and dominance

Together we are strong: to live in social groups has many advantages. When individuals cooperate, they can, for example, catch prey they wouldn't otherwise be able to handle. Just think about the wolf pack that catches an elk weighing ten times as much as a single wolf.

But the advantages of cooperation between animals don't always have to be about food. Cooperation can also be important when it comes to defending territory or raising cubs. The individuals in the group can divide the tasks between themselves and learn from one another's successes and failures. But living in a group can also take its toll. Not all individuals in the group might have a chance to procreate, and when food is lacking not everyone gets to fill their stomach. This could in turn lead to long-term stress and conflicts that result in physical fights. That's when it's particularly important to maintain the hierarchy of the group.

In groups of capuchin monkeys in South America, for example, some individuals are more dominant than others, and there's a clear hierarchy. When two individuals meet, they clearly show their status in the hierarchy through dominant or submissive signals. Sometimes the expressions seem strange; for example, a dominant individual will put its finger into a submissive monkey's nostril or eye. The monkeys constantly test each other in order to maintain the hierarchy within the group.

Dogs also show behaviours that signal dominance or submissiveness but their importance in maintaining relationships within the group is still controversial among researchers. A team led by John Bradshaw studied 19 neutered male dogs at a dogs' home and found no evidence to suggest a hierarchical division between individuals. It was, in other words, not always the case that some individuals were always the top rank and others always the lowest. Their status depended on the situation and the occasion.

Bradshaw and his colleagues therefore argue that behaviour signalling status doesn't work to describe social relationships, at least not with neutered pet dogs. An explanation could be that most dogs today don't live in packs; therefore it's not as important to display behaviours that show dominance and submissiveness. Another explanation could be that aggressive behaviour is generally less common among neutered dogs.

More articles published in the past few years have studied in detail dogs' behaviour in groups, and the conclusions differ from what Bradshaw and his colleagues imply. In one of these articles, the American researchers Rebecca Trisko and Barbara Smuts studied 12 male and 12 female dogs at a dog daycare centre. The dogs were from different breeds, but all had been neutered. From interactions between different combinations of dogs, the researchers found that submissive behaviour was much more common than dominant behaviour. The most common submissive signal was when a dog in a low position licked the corner of the mouth of a more dominant dog.

This and other behaviours varied according to the situation and occasion. In other words, there was a clear hierarchical structure among most individuals at the dog daycare centre, and this was stable from day to day. Older dogs had higher rank than younger ones, regardless of their body size, so smaller, older dogs often had a higher rank than larger, younger dogs.

Just as in earlier studies of wolves, dominant behaviours were more common in interactions between the same gender than between genders. Not all dogs 'fell into line', however. Some individuals' status varied from day to day. A dog's personality also seemed to be a more important factor in their ranking than which breed they belonged to. But the researchers pointed out that the sample was too limited to find out whether certain dog breeds were more dominant than others. They also note that we don't know today how much dog breeds with very different appearances understand each other's behaviours.

Maybe similar-looking dogs understand each other better? Because there are differences in appearance and temperament between dog breeds, shouldn't we expect a clearer hierarchy – that is, clear differences in rank between individuals – in more 'brash' dog breeds compared to the more 'shy' ones? Compare, for example, the more forward and extrovert personalities of Rottweilers and Belgian Shepherds with the more laid-back traits of Cavalier King Charles Spaniels and Labrador Retrievers. To find out if this is the case, we first have to know whether there are any general behaviours that signal status within a group of dogs with different ranks.

A Dutch research team published such a study in 2015 in *PloS ONE*. Joanne van der Borg and her colleagues tested 24 very different behaviours and seven different body postures (see the tables below) to determine which of them best describe differences in status. The researchers had the assistance of ten dogs in a newly established kennel at the University of Utrecht in the Netherlands. Male as well as female dogs from different breeds were included in the study and none of the dogs was neutered. The researchers studied paired interactions between these dogs for over 300 hours. For a behaviour to signal status in a reliable way, the researchers set up criteria: it should be displayed often in paired interactions, but only one of the dogs was to display the behaviour, and a stable pecking order was to be established between dogs from this behaviour.

The dog to the right shows its lower status in the hierarchy by licking the corner of the mouth of the more dominant dog while keeping its body in a low position.

The following table shows the actions that most clearly signal submissive or dominant behaviours according to Dutch research. The list of terms below the table collects behaviours that cannot be so easily categorised one way or the other.

BEHAVIOUR	SUBMISSIVE OR DOMINANT?	DESCRIPTION
Lick mouth	*Submissive*	Repeatedly licks the corner of the receiver's mouth with quick movements
Body and tail wag	*Submissive*	Wags its tail irregularly and quickly; often the back moves too; low or neutral posture
Walk past under the head	*Submissive*	Comes from the side and passes the recipient's head with brief contact nose to cheek; low or neutral posture
Flee	*Submissive*	Runs at least 3 metres from the recipient, with head facing away from the recipient
Lash out	*Dominant*	Bites the air as the dog moves 1 or 2 steps towards the recipient; no physical contact
Stand above	*Dominant*	Holds head above recipient's body, four paws on the ground, in a neutral or high posture
Bite nose	*Dominant*	Nibbles the recipient's nose from above or the side

Stare, Hackles raised, Growl, Show teeth, Lunge, Bite, Fight, Fall back, Retreat, Lick their nose, Look away, Freeze, Approach, Steal objects, Bark, Wag the tail, Paw on top.

This table for seven different body postures shows actions that are less reliable for indicating dominance or submission.

POSTURE	TAIL	EARS
High	As high as possible	As high up or as forward as possible
Half-high	Above the level of the back	Partly upwards or ahead, higher than neutral
Neutral	Follows the back of the body, just below the level of the back	Relaxed
On its back	Like neutral posture but with the dog on its back or side	Like neutral posture but with the dog on its back or side
Half-low	Lower than neutral but not against or between hind legs	Partly low or ahead, lower than neutral
Low	S-shaped and against the back of the body, or between hind legs	As low or as far back as possible
Low, on its back	Like low posture but with the dog on its back or side	Like low posture

Of all the 24 behaviours, it was the 'body/tail wag' that best fitted these criteria. This ritualized behaviour signals clear submissiveness and friendly intentions towards the recipient. 'Mouth lick' and 'Walk past under the head' were also clear submissive signals that were used only for the top-ranking male and female dog. It wasn't as easy to find behaviours signalling dominance, but 'Bite nose' was something only dogs of the highest rank carried out on their 'subjects'. All behaviours are clearly followed by a certain body posture that strengthens the message.

The researchers could show a clear submissive signal if a dog changed its posture from 'higher' to 'lower' when it interacted with a dominant dog (see the table above). Van der Borg and her colleagues could also show a clear pecking order between the ten dogs. If a dog didn't understand its place in the pack, a dominant dog would usually express displeasure by staring, showing its teeth or lunging towards the submissive animal.

This mild form of aggression made the dogs in this group display a tolerant dominant relationship, according to the researchers. If differences in rank are particularly large between the lead dog and the others, researchers usually call that a domineering relationship. By contrast, when the differences are small or negligible, they call the dominance relationship relaxed or equal.

The hierarchy between dogs can become particularly clear when female dogs are on heat and when they are suckling puppies. A study of stray dogs in India by Sunil Kumar Pal showed this. During the end of the monsoon, when the female dogs were on heat, aggressive behaviour between male dogs in the group was particularly common. And when the female dogs lactated, submissive behaviours towards the female dogs were the most common. The domination relationships within the group weren't as clear during other periods of the year.

The studies above also demonstrated that even neutered dogs show these dominant and submissive ritualized behaviours to show their status within a group – whether, for example, at the kennels, the dog daycare centre or the dog club.

SCIENTISTS EXPLAIN

Hierarchy and dominance

- To 'know your place' reduces the risk of conflict between members of social groups.
- Several studies show that dogs living in groups often organize themselves into a hierarchy, where some are dominant and others submissive. The behaviours that most clearly signal submissiveness are: (1) wagging the tail when the body is in a low posture; (2) licking the mouth of the receiver; (3) walking past under the head of the receiver; and (4) changing the body posture from a higher to a lower position.
- The behaviour that signals dominance most clearly is to bite the receiver's nose.
- Older dogs are usually more dominant than younger ones, regardless of size.
- Aggressive interactions are more common within the same gender.
- Relationships of dominance within a group are expected to vary depending on the breed composition of the dogs.
- The most common relationships within dog groups are so-called tolerant dominance relationships, rather than despotic or equal dominance relationships.

2

The dog–human relationship

HOW ARE YOU going to get your new faithful servant to bond with you? And does your dog behave differently towards you than towards your friends or strangers? In this chapter, you'll read researchers' answers to these questions. We will also look closely at how dogs can contribute to humans having a better and healthier life. Did you know, for example, that the market for assistance and service dogs has grown enormously in the past few years?

Bonding

It's finally time to get a dog! You have chosen a puppy from a well-known breeder, read several books about raising dogs, and booked classes on a puppy course. You've done everything right. But there is still a worry gnawing at you after a few weeks with your new puppy – has my companion in life really bonded with me as it should have? Maybe I should do something differently to get an even better connection?

Researchers call the interaction between you and your dog 'dyadic', because you are a pair and it's as much up to you as it's up to your dog to develop the desirable, tight bond that allows your puppy to develop into a confident individual. In this chapter you will read as much about yourself and your behaviour as you will about your puppy and its behaviour.

A good and secure connection is the basis for a happy and tranquil dog, leaving it with enough energy to discover and explore its environment. In a way, the dog's desire to bond with its owner can be described as a survival instinct. The pet dog needs a human to meet its basic needs – such as food and shelter – but it also needs its relationship with the human to protect it against real and imagined dangers. Bonding is about your dog feeling safe: your pet needs to know that you will look after it and offer it protection and food (rather than being merely a fun playmate).

But how can you determine whether your dog really has bonded with you in a good way? To find out, researchers in ethology – the scientific study of animal behaviour – have started from the same four theories that psychologists usually use to describe the degree of bonding between children and their parents, namely 'secure base', 'safe haven', 'separation distress' and 'proximity maintenance'.

The Australian researcher Elyssa Payne and her colleagues published an overview article in the journal *Behavioural Processes*, for which they had gone through earlier published articles to see what support the four theories had in science. The results showed that the best sign of your dog having bonded with you in a positive way is if it plays and explores more when you are present compared to when it's alone or with strangers. You are then the dog's 'secure base' – you make the dog feel safe enough to explore its surroundings and investigate unknown objects.

Another sign of strong bonding that is almost as good is if your dog comes to you when it feels anxious, for example if a threatening stranger approaches. This indicates that you are your dog's 'safe harbour' in stressful situations. Payne and her colleagues could, among other things, show that the dog's pulse didn't increase in the same way when the owner was present as when it was alone. That dogs can suffer from separation anxiety when their owners leave them on their own is well established in many studies.

Another indication of good bonding is believed to be the behaviour a dog displays when reunited with its owner after being on its own in a strange environment. But what does it mean if your dog is excessive in its search for closeness and is attached to you like a sticking plaster? This is not necessarily to be regarded as a success in developing a safe bonding relationship. Payne and her colleagues noted that, when owners reported a very close bond with their dogs, the dogs in turn showed a greater need for closeness with the owners. The researchers speculate that, if the dog mirrors the owner's personality and behaviour too closely, it may become more anxious and less independent than it would be otherwise.

But so far no study has been able to say for sure that 'seeking closeness' has its basis in anxious behaviour. Even dogs in rehoming centres seek closeness with complete strangers after a short introduction. Therefore it doesn't have to be a dog's need to seek the owner's proximity that shows a close bond. In other words, it seems that the safest indications of a close bond between dog and owner is what the researchers call 'a secure base' and 'safe haven'. As a dog owner, you need to be sensitive to your dog, and your job is to show that things aren't dangerous. Having a secure bond has a lot to do with you as an owner tuning in and reading your dog to meet its needs. But how do you go about achieving this close bond and a good relationship with your dog?

It's probable that a person who is perceptive and empathic towards other people will also understand their dog's behaviour more easily. Do you remember the term 'emotional intelligence' that was so popular over 20 years ago? The psychologist and science journalist Daniel Goleman coined the phrase to describe a person's ability to read their own and others' emotions. Emotional intelligence consists of five elements: self-awareness, self-control, driving force motivation, empathy and social ability.

Many things point to these abilities in dog owners being a determining factor in how strong the bond between dog and human becomes. If the owner shows a high EQ – short for emotional quotient in the same way that IQ is short for intelligence quotient – it ought to be reflected in a better relationship between human and animal. However, Payne and her colleagues state that little research has been done to show whether EQ could contribute to a better bond.

What we do know is that empathetic dog owners with a positive attitude have less stressed dogs – as measured by the amount of stress hormone cortisol in the saliva. An empathetic dog owner sees their dog as a friend and often has an emotional tie that helps them identify signs of pain or distress in their dog. A more dominant owner who judges their dog by their 'usefulness' tries more often to force their dog to obey their will.

When your dog behaves well, giving positive feedback makes it easier to bond with your pet or confirm an already good relationship. You probably already know the tricks: food, physical contact and play. However, dogs seem to prefer rewards like food or treats to being stroked or brushed. In fact, researchers aren't afraid to say that food is the determining factor for a good bond between dog and human. It is mainly dogs that are starved of physical contact – as dogs in rehoming centres might be – that appreciate being stroked or brushed more than pet dogs.

Playing with your dog is another way to strengthen ties and it is also a good way of decreasing stress in your dog. And the dog's need to play with its owner doesn't decrease just because it has the opportunity to play with other dogs. Playing with humans seems to fulfil a different need in the dog from playing with other dogs (see 'Dog play' in Chapter 1).

Another useful way to have a positive relationship is to give your dog praise for good behaviour. The American researchers Erica Feuerbacher and Clive Wynne wanted to find out whether dogs preferred an encouraging pat or verbal praise. Their conclusion comes from the article's unmistakable title: 'Shut up and pet me!' In the study the researchers used 42 dogs in 14 rehoming centres with strangers, 14 pet dogs with their owners, and 14 pet dogs with strangers. Regardless of their background, all the dogs preferred to be patted on the body part closest to the human rather than receiving verbal praise such as 'You're such a good dog. You're so cute!' spoken in a happy voice.

The verbal praise didn't seem to have any effect on the dogs, because they didn't stay with the humans any longer than they did when people sat passively in silence. The contrast was striking, however, when the dogs were patted for three minutes. None of them showed any signs of having had enough during those three minutes. Physical contact was therefore found to be better for bonding with dogs than giving verbal praise.

Dogs have a unique relationship with humans and are often seen as family members. In a large American study from 1999, 84 per cent of the dog owners asked considered themselves to be the dog's mother or father rather than its owner. The step from there to anthropomorphizing the dog – assuming that the dog's behaviour is controlled by motives resembling the human's – doesn't have to be that big.

Modern behavioural science is critical, however, of seeing in animal behaviour human emotions such as happiness, sorrow, jealousy and shame. It is not a sign of guilt or shame if a dog avoids eye contact after it has destroyed your beautiful china. It's actually a learned behaviour and a response to your reaction. We send out conscious or subconscious signals and our dogs reply with behaviour that shows submissiveness. This is not the dog consciously realizing its mistake.

But it's still easy to fall into the trap of projecting our own emotions on to dogs. The American psychologists Christina Brown and Julia McLean have shown that humans who are inclined to often feel guilt in their own life were more likely to think that their dogs were ashamed after they'd done something silly. In the same way, these people also assume that active dogs are afraid or anxious, despite there being no clear threat to them, when they pace back and forth in front of a door.

We always tell our children that it's what's on the inside that counts. We think it's superficial to judge other people by appearances. But are we less judgemental when it comes to dogs? Do we think that appealing-looking dogs have a better personality than ugly dogs? We might also believe that cute dogs bond better with us than ugly dogs. This was something that a research team led by Pinar Thorn from Australia investigated, by asking about 700 dog owners on the Internet how strong their bond was with their dogs, based on 28 questions.

The owners also described the dogs' personality from another 26 questions, which could be summarized in five dimensions: friendly, extroverted, motivated, neurotic and focused on training. Finally, the owners described how cute they thought their dogs were on a six-point scale: 'not cute at all' to 'very cute'. The results showed that the owners who believed their dogs were cute had also bonded with them to a higher degree. And 'cuteness' was as important as personality for the owners to have a good bond with the dogs.

But beauty seems to be in the eye of the beholder. Almost 900 people who didn't know the dogs that were assessed in the study got to judge from a photograph how cute they thought the dogs were. It turned out that almost without exception they thought the dogs were uglier than the owners believed. But, just like the owners, these people thought that cute dogs were friendlier than ugly dogs, despite never having met the dogs in real life. It's obvious, then, that we judge the dog by its fur.

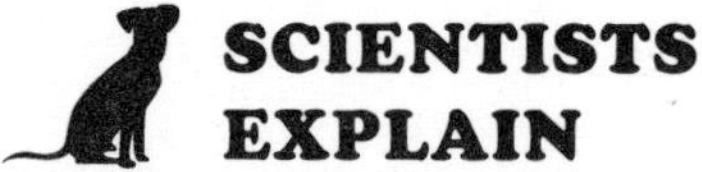

Bonding

- Researchers call the interaction between you and your dog 'dyadic' to describe that it's as much up to you as it's up to your dog to make the bond between you good.
- According to bonding theory, a good bond between you and your dog can manifest itself when the dog seeks shelter with you when a threatening stranger approaches (safe harbour) or when it plays/explores more in your presence (safe base).
- To establish a close bond, giving your dog positive feedback through food, physical contact and play when it shows good behaviour works really well.
- Physical contact through stroking the dog is better for bonding than verbal praise.

How does your dog feel about you?

You expect your dog to be friendly and tolerant towards the new acquaintances it meets, both outdoors – when, for example, are out for a walk or during dog training – and indoors when you have friends visiting. But does your dog behave differently towards you compared to how it behaves towards your close friends or complete strangers? Maybe your dog only tolerates your close friends or strangers in certain situations? And where is the limit to how intimate a stranger can become with your dog?

A Hungarian research team led by Andrea Kerepsi investigated how 20 pet dogs interacted with their owners, the owners' close friends and complete strangers. Only women participated in the study because earlier studies had shown that many dogs act differently towards men than towards women, but also because research has shown that women interact with dogs differently from men. The dogs participated in eight different situations in total, as described in detail in the table below.

It was clear that only the owner was good enough in situations that tested bonding or separation anxiety – what's described in the table as 'unknown situation', 'go away' or 'threatening approach'. It's the owner who is the dog's secure base when something bad happens, and it's the owner that the dog misses when she temporarily moves out of sight. Also when playing, the dog regards its owner as a much better playmate than their close friend or the stranger.

The dog didn't differentiate, however, between its owner and the close friend when it came to obedience exercises – what's described in the table below as 'call the dog from its food', 'obedience', 'no to the food' and 'manipulate the dog's body'. It's probably not unthinkable that her close friend had participated in earlier obedience exercises with the dog because it was a requirement of the study that they had socialized regularly, at least twice a week, for a long time. The dogs' limit seems to have been drawn at the manipulation exercise – the dogs didn't feel comfortable with anyone but their owner trying to put them on their back with their hands. The researchers were surprised that the difference between how dogs perceived the owner's close friends and complete strangers was so small.

SITUATION	EXPLANATION	THE RESEARCHERS' MEASURE
Unknown situation	In the centre of a room are three chairs with their backs against each other. In front of each chair are a ball and a chew toy. Three doors lead into the room. The dog is alone with the stranger, then with all three (owner, owner's close friend, complete stranger).	How long did the dog spend in contact or playing with any of the three people? How long did the dog wait by any of the doors?

(*Continued*)

Call the dog from its food	A piece of food is placed in a cage in front of the three people. The dog gets a taste and then the people call the dog at the same time for 30 seconds.	How long was the dog turned towards each person? How often did it look between the food and each person?
Obedience	The three people stand in a semicircle in front of the dog. Each one tries to make the dog lie down for 15 seconds.	Did the people succeed or not? How long did it take them?
Go away	The three people go away from the dog without glancing at it. When they are 5 metres away, one goes to the left, another straight on and the third to the right.	Which of the people did the dog follow (three attempts)?
Threatening approach	The three people stand in a semicircle with the dog in the centre. A fourth person wearing a dark raincoat with a hood approaches slowly and limps towards the dog, while staring silently into its eyes.	Which of the people did the dog approach?

(*Continued*)

Playful interaction	The three people stand facing away from the dog, 5 metres away. A fourth person throws a ball and when the dog catches the ball in its mouth the other three try to make the dog come to one of them.	How long was the dog turned to each person? To whom did the dog go with the ball?
No to the food	The three people stand in a semicircle with the dog on a lead in the centre. A piece of sausage is attached on a disc to each person's leg. The dog is led to each one and when it catches the scent, the person says 'No!' The dog is then released.	In what order did the dog approach the people when it was set free and how long did it take before it tried to take the food?
Manipulate the dog's body	The three people try to make the dog sit, lie still and roll on its back. They aren't allowed to use commands to make the dog move into position, but must use their hands.	How many times did they manage to make the dog do each move for 15 seconds?

This experiment tested how pet dogs interact with their owner, the owners' close friend and a complete stranger when put in eight different situations.

Since most socialized pet dogs will have had only positive experiences of meeting all sorts of strangers, they will accept them more easily in obedience exercises. But if a dog becomes really frightened or worried, it comes to its owner for comfort and closeness. An important conclusion of this study is that a dog's behaviour and motivation will vary depending on whether or not its owner is present.

For some reason it seems that dogs in dogs' homes prefer female to male staff. They bark less, yawn more often and have a more relaxed posture in the vicinity of women and they prefer to approach women rather than men. The New Zealand researchers Min Hooi Yong and Ted Ruffman suggest that dogs in general are more watchful towards men than women. They think that dogs are conditioned to react less positively to (men's) deeper, lower-frequency voices because they signal danger. We all know that dogs lower their tone and growl deeply when something threatening approaches or if another dog tries to steal their food.

That's why researchers believe that dogs take a more defensive stance and are more watchful of men, at least men they haven't previously met. The 45 dogs participating in the New Zealand study had to try to match a female or a male voice – reading a nonsense sentence: 'Hat sundig pron you vency' in a neutral voice – with photographs of men and women with neutral expressions shown on a monitor. It turned out that the dogs in the experiment managed to match the male voices with the photographs of men, but they failed to match female voices with photographs of women. And this result stood regardless of the dog's gender or age. The researchers interpreted this as support for the hypothesis that dogs are more watchful when they hear men's deeper voices.

In an exciting study published in 2016 in the magazine *Biology Letters*, a research team led by Natalia Albuquerque demonstrated that dogs also understand how humans feel. You as a dog owner maybe think it's obvious that your dog can interpret your feelings, but in this case the level of difficulty was much higher than that! The 17 dogs participating in the experiment heard an unknown person say one word in a language that was foreign to the dogs. The words were either spoken with an angry or a happy voice. To allow for the fact that dogs perceive men and women differently, one man and one woman uttered the same word. Then the dogs got five seconds to match the angry or the happy voice with black-and-white photographs of an angry or happy woman or man.

The researchers recorded the dogs. When the dogs kept their gaze on the photograph of a happy person when they heard a happy voice for a longer time, or on an angry person when they heard an angry voice, the researchers interpreted this as the dog understanding the point. The dogs didn't receive any further clues and they couldn't interpret the situation from something that happened or use their superior sense of smell.

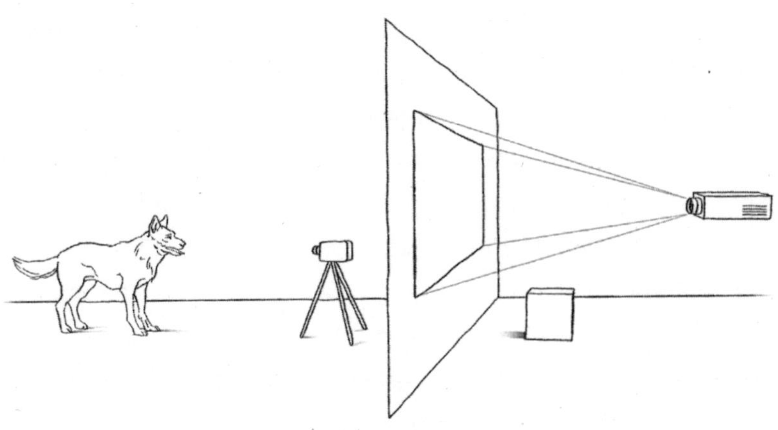

Dogs understand our moods exceptionally well. From only one word, spoken with an angry or a happy voice, the dogs managed to match the emotion with black-and-white photographs of an angry or happy woman or man.

A loudspeaker behind the screen said the word, and after that photographs of two faces were shown on the screen for five seconds. A video camera in front of the dog documented which of the two faces the dog looked at for longest.

Despite the dogs not being able to use all their senses, they matched the correct face with the correct mood far often than might be explained by random chance. And it didn't matter whether it was a woman or a man who said the word: the dogs managed equally well with both genders. In contrast to the New Zealand study mentioned earlier, the dogs were better at matching voices to the correct gender when emotions were added, compared to when voices were neutral.

This study is ground-breaking because it's the first time researchers have shown that animals understand humans' moods almost as well as we understand them ourselves. But no one is surprised that dogs have developed the ability to understand our emotions just from listening: they need to be able to understand humans because they live most of their lives closer to us than to their own species.

Exactly the same set-up as above was used in another experiment by the same research team, but this time the participating dogs listened to the sound of a dog being playful or aggressive. The dogs then had to try to match these sounds with black-and-white photographs of a playful or an angry dog. They obviously managed to solve this task brilliantly, even a little better than when analysing humans' moods.

Dogs live a socially rich life alongside humans. They study our faces carefully to receive guidance on what they should do in various situations, and they can distinguish their owner's close friend from an acquaintance or a complete stranger. They can also understand our emotions from our different facial expressions. But how does their brain manage to distinguish different human faces and emotions?

With the help of magnetic resonance imaging, researchers can see how the brain works while a dog is solving a task. Oxygenated blood flows to various parts of the brain, which 'light up' on the images. A Mexican research team led by Laura Cuaya managed the feat of teaching seven dogs – five Border

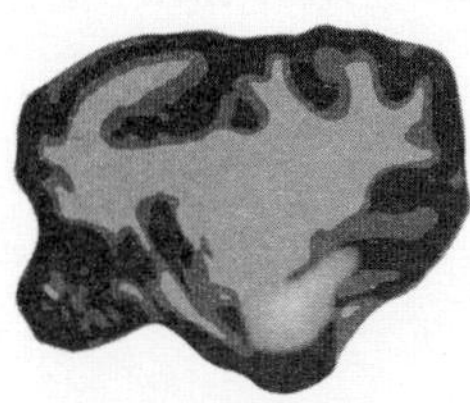

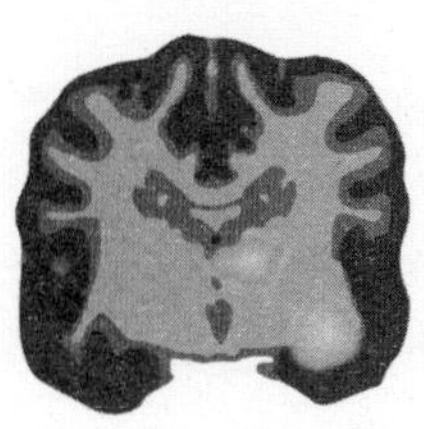

Now we're able to 'see' how a dog thinks! By using magnetic resonance imaging (MRI) (above) we can see that the dog, just like the human, uses its brain's temporal lobe to remember different human faces.

When a dog sees photographs of human faces, oxygenated blood flows to its temporal lobe and we can clearly see the increased activity in the dog's brain from the front (lower left) and from the side (above left). When the dog sees photographs of everyday objects, the temporal lobe doesn't light up.

Collies, one Labrador Retriever and one Golden Retriever – to stay absolutely still in the scanner while the dogs looked at 50 photographs of human faces with neutral expressions and 50 photographs of various everyday objects.

The results showed that primarily the temporal lobe lit up when the dogs looked at the photographs of human faces.

However, they couldn't see any particular brain activity being registered when photographs of everyday objects were shown to the dogs. In humans it's also the temporal lobe that is activated when we see other faces. This part of the brain reacts twice as fast when we see faces compared to other visual stimuli.

With the help of this technology, we know today that both humans and dogs mainly use the brain's temporal lobe to remember different faces. This research is still in its infancy and there are definitely going to be more exciting uses for the technology in the future to help us 'see' when dogs are thinking!

How does your dog feel about you?

- A dog's behaviour and motivation vary depending on whether or not its owner is present.
- Dogs don't distinguish between owners and their close friends when it comes to obedience practice. If a situation is experienced as threatening, it's only the owner who works as the dog's safe base.
- Dogs distinguish women from men. They're generally more watchful towards men than women.
- As far as we know today, the dog is the only animal that understands our moods almost as well as we understand them ourselves.

Assistance and service dogs

In 79 CE the town of Pompeii was buried in ash and mud by the Vesuvius volcano eruption. When archaeologists excavated the town, they found a wall painting of a blind man with a stick being led by a dog. This is very first documentation of a guide dog. Obviously, dogs have been helping humans with various disabilities for millennia, but it's only in the past hundred years that we have systematically trained dogs to assist us in different ways. And during the 2000s the number of functions the dog fulfils in our service has massively increased, as shown in the boxes given a little later in this chapter.

Assistance dogs help people with various disabilities to live a freer life. Improved opportunities to meet people often lead to increased self-esteem and better self-confidence. The guide dog's status has increased dramatically during recent decades, and these highly trained dogs are usually allowed to go anywhere with their owner.

In the UK over 7,000 disabled people rely on an assistance dog to help with practical tasks – offering emotional support and independence. Assistance Dogs UK (ADUK) is a coalition of eight assistance dog charities, which provides a kite-mark of excellence in assistance dog training. All ADUK dogs adhere to the highest training and welfare standards as set out by Assistance Dogs International and the International Guide Dogs Federation.

However, in the USA there is no requirement for a certificate or licence that documents that a guide dog has had adequate training for the task. And unfortunately there have been several incidents where guide dogs have injured people in the USA. Legislation has simply not caught up with progress. In an article published in 2015 in *PLoS ONE,* A group of researchers led by Mariko Yamamoto from California described the situation regarding guide dogs in the USA as close to chaotic.

Service, therapy and assistance dogs perform a variety of functions, as follows:

Service dogs

Service dogs work within the police, surveillance companies, in criminal justice, customs, the military and emergency services. Other than search-and-rescue and patrol dogs, there are also specialist dogs used to search for narcotics and in mines.

- **Rescue dogs** seek and identify people who have been buried, for example after earthquakes or avalanches.
- **Patrol dogs** work with the armed forces to alert their handlers in surveillance areas. These dogs mark sounds or follow tracks on the ground to reveal people hiding in the terrain.

Therapy dogs

Therapy dogs are trained to increase a person's motivation, wellbeing and/or health. Together with its handler, the dog may work as support and help for several people.

- **Visiting therapy dogs** visit people simply to lend support, to help motivate and encourage activity, and provide company. They may work according to an action plan with set targets to give this support and improve motivation.
- **Care dogs** work in elderly care, dementia care and in the rehabilitation of people with a brain injury.
- **Educational therapy dogs** work in schools or other educational environments to help encourage students to develop their reading comprehension and other skills. They are also called school dogs, pedagogy dogs or sponsor dogs.
- **Cancer dogs** have been trained to use their sense of smell to identify cancer in people, for example through breathing samples (lung cancer, breast cancer), urine samples (prostate cancer) or tissue samples (ovarian cancer)

Assistance dogs

Assistant dogs are used as aids for a specific handler with a certain chronic disability or disease.

- **A guide dog** helps a person with a visual impairment to avoid obstacles, stop at stairs and pavement edges, and look for benches and so on.

- **An assistance/disability dog** helps a person with a disability to, for example, open doors, pick up a telephone, or send an alarm if the person needs medical assistance.
- **A hearing dog** helps someone with a hearing impairment by marking certain sounds, for example a smoke alarm or a telephone ringing.
- **Medical detection dogs** warn their handler before his/her health worsens, for example if their blood-sugar level becomes too low if they are diabetic or before an epileptic seizure.

This information was mostly sourced from the Swedish Kennel Club and Swedish Dogs Club.

What breed makes the best assistance or service dog? There are almost 5,000 trained guide dogs in the UK today, mainly Golden Retrievers or Labradors. What makes the Labrador so popular as a guide dog? It shouldn't really be the breed that determines whether a certain dog is appropriate or not; instead, it should be an individual dog's characteristics that are the determining factor.

An English research team, led by Fernanda Ruiz Fadel, published an exciting article in *Scientific Reports* in 2016, which helps to puncture the myth of breed-typical behaviours and characteristics. The researchers created an elegant experiment comparing the behaviour of Labrador Retrievers and Border

Collies that had been bred for working and show purposes. The behaviours in more than a thousand dogs were analysed with the help of a dog owner survey called DIAS – the Dog Impulsivity Assessment Scale.

In line with expectations of the working dogs, the 'herding dog' Border Collie was more impulsive than the 'hunting dog' Labrador Retriever. But with the show dogs there were no differences in behaviour between the Border Collie and the Labrador Retriever. The results also showed that differences in behaviour *within* breeds – between working dogs and show dogs – was larger than the differences *between* breeds. So it's not the breed that determines whether or not a dog is appropriate as a guide dog. The researchers conclude with a clear recommendation: 'Our results show that generalizations based on breed are not appropriate.'

Please also compare this with what I write in Chapter 6 – with regard to the sense of smell – about other discoveries that question established 'truths'. But how are we then going to get any guidance on which individual dog fits a certain task best? It no longer appears that certain breeds are always appropriate for specific guiding or assistance tasks. Maybe we can get some help from the puppy personality tests (see Chapter 1)? Unfortunately, they don't seem to be particularly reliable either, at least not for puppies younger than 12 weeks.

It seems, however, that the tests become more accurate when the puppies reach around six months old. That's why an English research team led by Naomi D. Harvey tested the behaviour of dogs participating in guide dog training at the age of five months. They tested the same dogs again when they were eight months old, to see if they reacted in the same way. A total of 93 dogs did the training and most of them were Labrador Retrievers or crosses between Labrador and Golden Retrievers. The researchers were particularly curious to see whether any of the tests could predict which dogs would be able to complete the training.

Out of the 93 dogs in the study, 61 completed the training, while 22 left early because of one or more unwanted behaviours. Four dogs left for health reasons, and six others became breeding dogs instead. The researchers managed to predict which dogs would complete the training or leave prematurely in 80 per cent of the cases at five months old, and in 87 per cent of the cases at eight months old.

You can read a simplified version of the evaluation in the table below. Considering that the evaluation only took 20 minutes to conduct, this must be seen as money well spent; the lifetime cost of training a guide dog, from birth to retirement, is around £55,000. More important than that is the dogs' wellbeing. Dogs that become stressed by the training in various ways should become pets instead. Unlike guide dogs, service dogs are trained for tasks that aren't tied to a specific handler.

As we have seen, the areas in which dogs are used as assistance and service animals are increasing. When service dogs are at work, they will meet many unknown people and situations that can be stressful and cause them anxiety. That is why it is so important to ensure that these dogs have a stable and reliable temperament. They must be able to tolerate strangers approaching them in a threatening way, sudden loud noises and shouts, and being handled roughly. After their training is complete,

EVALUATION/TEST	WHAT DOES THE EVALUATION SHOW?
A plate of sausages is placed in the dog's vicinity. The handler calls the dog by saying 'Come, [dog's name]' and 'Go' in turn.	Shows the dog's willingness to obey despite the lure of food.
The owner gives the command 'Lie down!' Does the dog obey straight away? A stranger gives the dog the same command – does the dog obey on the second or the third attempt?	Shows the dog's willingness to obey.
A towel is placed on the dog's back.	Shows whether the dog will accept wearing a service jacket.
Two stuffed birds (a robin and a wood pigeon) are placed in the vicinity of the leashed dog.	Shows whether the dog is distracted (either frightened or lured) by other animals.

If the dog barked, licked its lips or trembled during any of these tests, they were seen as signs of fear or anxiety.

guide dogs and service dogs must be assessed regularly to ensure that their behaviours don't deteriorate with age. It's like an MoT, where the roadworthiness of older cars is checked each year.

An Italian research group led by Paolo Mongillo used both role-play and behavioural tests to evaluate the continued suitability of 40 service dogs as against 20 pet dogs. The dogs were divided into three groups from the test answers: 'suitable' (equivalent of a pass on the MoT), 'suitable with reservations' (not passed the MoT) and finally 'not suitable at all' (taken off the road). The 'MoT' showed that only 3 out of 40 service dogs were 'taken off the road' and that the handlers already felt this would happen before the test was conducted. In other words, a yearly inspection gives a good indication of whether a dog should retire or continue. In contrast, of the tested pet dogs, 15 out of 20 were 'taken off the road'.

But it's not always easy to evaluate whether a dog is appropriate for certain tasks. Patrol dogs that work for the police or the military are often exposed to stressful or threatening situations. They must be able to be focused and unafraid during a work shift, which may last for several hours.

Pernilla Foyer and her colleagues at the University in Linköping, Sweden, investigated how stressed German Shepherds, training to become patrol dogs, were in four different test situations, partly by studying video recordings of behavioural tests in detail, and partly by measuring the stress hormone cortisol in the 37 dogs before and after the tests. The researchers didn't know which dogs the test leaders had approved or not approved for further training. Surprisingly, the German Shepherds that had been accepted showed clear signs of anxiety and had higher stress levels than the dogs that had not been accepted.

The same research team showed in an earlier study that German Shepherds that had passed the behaviour tests had difficulties calming down afterwards and showed signs of hyperactivity. That's not a good attribute in a patrol dog, which has to relax when the work is finished, and then quickly start again when it's time to return to work.

Do these results mean that there are systematic errors in the education of military dogs? Or do the results show more that dogs displaying a broader emotional register are more 'on it' and therefore pass the training better? In all likelihood, further research from the team in Linköping will present answers in the near future.

People who have the disorder autism have difficulties taking in a lot of information at the same time, and in socializing and communicating with others. Rituals and stereotypical behaviours often have a calming effect, and sometimes people with autism have special interests that overshadow everything else.

Two studies from England investigated how dogs could help people with autism function better in their everyday life. There are trained therapy dogs for people with autism, but in these studies they didn't use dogs that were specially trained for the purpose. Instead, the first study evaluated the effect of a therapy dog on three students with autism, and the second study evaluated the effect of pet dogs on children with autism.

The study showed that all three students had more meaningful interactions with their teacher after the dog came into their lives, and the number of stereotypical, repeated behaviours decreased. The researchers conclude that therapy dogs motivate students with autism to become more receptive to their surroundings, thereby strengthening their social relationships. The English study also found that pet dogs can contribute to children with autism having a richer life. The results were particularly good if the parents had participated in the workshops that PAWS (Dogs for Good Parents Autism Workshops) had arranged, and if the family got a dog when their autistic child was more than eight years old.

Lastly in this section, I'd like to tell you about the clever technical gadget à la *Mission Impossible* that is coming up for assistance dogs. It's project FIDO – 'Facilitating Interactions for Dogs with Occupations' – which offers a vest with different sensors to aid the dogs in communicating with their handler. The primed service dog can, with the help of the vest, call 999 when the owner is having an epileptic seizure; the service dog can show in plain text on the vest's display that a fire alarm is going off; the rescue dog can send GPS coordinates directly to the handler's mobile phone when it has found a lost child. The possibilities are endless!

And today it's not about the dogs' ability to learn that limits their usefulness, but the longevity of a battery and how small and strong it's possible to make the vest's sensors. A lot of work is still to be done, but FIDO has shown that these vests aren't in any way science fiction!

Technological advances make it possible for assistance and guide dogs to wear a vest with sensors that enables them to communicate better with us, for example by calling 999 if their handler has an epileptic seizure.

SCIENTISTS EXPLAIN

Assistance and service dogs

- Since the year 2000 the number of functions the dog fulfils in our service has massively increased.
- Assistance dogs are generally classified as guide dogs, disability dogs or hearing dogs.
- It's not the dog breed in itself that determines how appropriate it is for certain tasks. Instead, it's the individual characteristics of a particular animal.
- From certain behavioural experiments, it's possible to determine which dogs are more suitable to undertake guide dog training.

- Service dogs and guide dogs should go through regular yearly tests to determine whether or not the dog should be retired.
- Guide and hearing dogs are in service for about eight years.
- An assistance or service dog in action or in training should wear a service jacket.
- Therapy dogs can help people with Alzheimer's disease or autism to be more receptive to the outside world and have a richer social life.

Healthy dog walks

We may not always be patient when our dog wants to sniff a little longer or pee one more time; instead we pull the lead impatiently and tell the dog to keep moving. But maybe it's possible to combine giving our dog exercise and meeting its needs with our own exercise? At least that's an idea permeating many recent scientific studies. The context for this is that dogs as well as humans are afflicted by so-called lifestyle diseases as a result of being overweight.

Of the scientific studies published over the past few years, a large number have focused on the advantages of walking for the *dog owner*. But a newly published study shows the benefits for dogs: dogs that go on walks are less afraid of sudden noises than those that don't (see Chapter 4 on fear, worry and anxiety). So perhaps walks improve dogs' mental health and counteract anxiety in the same way that 'prescribed' daily walks for depressed people do? Another study from England showed that overweight dogs generally had *less* exercise than normal-weight dogs because they were less mobile and eager to play (see Chapter 5 on excess weight and obesity). Such a vicious circle is hard to break.

The UK government recommends that we get at least 30 minutes of exercise each day and this is something that everybody can achieve on a daily dog walk. Dogs' exercise needs vary according to the breed that you have but every dog should have at least one walk a day, often two. Use the Breed Information Centre on the UK Kennel Club's website to find out more about the exercise needs of your chosen breed. Is it better to go for several short walks than fewer long ones? Can I exercise my dog too much? How many walks can a puppy or an old dog cope with? There's room for more research here that could really benefit many dog owners in the future. The prerequisites for dog walks differ in different parts of the world.

Owners in the USA often release their dogs to roam freely in specific dog parks. The dog has a lot of exercise but the owner doesn't move as much. These parks are rare in Europe. An English research team led by Carri Westgarth recently conducted in-depth interviews of members of 260 dog households in Cheshire, near Liverpool. Fewer than 80 per cent of the dog owners took at least one daily dog walk lasting between 15 minutes and an hour. What influenced them to take the dog out daily was the number of dogs in the household. Dogs were less likely to be taken out on daily walks if there were more dogs in the home – and also if there were several people in the household. The researchers believe that it could be more difficult for owners to keep track of several dogs during a walk, which makes them unhappy about taking them out.

Another explanation could be that the dogs have the company of each other at home and the owners therefore don't think they need to go out to play with other dogs. Families with children don't seem to have time either to take their dog out as often as singles or couples without children. The most striking result of the research was that the bond between owner and dog determined how often they went out together. The chances of daily walks were greatly reduced if the dog growled at someone in the household.

Pensioners have more than one reason to get a dog. Lonely people especially can have a dear friend in their dog, and dog ownership makes it easier for them to break out of social isolation and go out and meet new people.

Another valuable reason is of course the increase in daily exercise. A sedentary lifestyle increases the risk of cardiovascular diseases and early death. American pensioners are advised to take at least 150 minutes of medium-intensive physical activity each week under guidelines from the US Department of Health. Today only half of America's pensioners are able to reach this level.

A study published in *Preventive Medicine* by David Garcia and his colleagues compared exercise habits in dog owners and non-dog owners in almost 150,000 women older than 60 in the USA. Not surprisingly, more dog owners than non-dog owners reached the guidelines of 150 minutes' exercise per week. Single women were particularly likely to go out with their dog more often. But perhaps more surprising was that older dog owners in general walked more slowly than non-dog owners. This might be because they are more afraid of falling if the dog pulls the lead, or because they stop more often so the dog can do what it should, or because they speak more with other dog owners.

Another group that would benefit from more exercise is teenagers. Imagine the joy many parents must have felt when their teenagers' changed their exercise habits in 2016. The reason was, of course, Pokémon Go, a game on your mobile phone where you chase virtual characters in 'the real world'. The game was just a fad, but could dog walks make teenagers continue exercising regularly?

The comparison with Pokémon isn't as far-fetched as it might seem. In a study of almost a thousand teenagers in the USA (the teenagers were actually between 12 and 17 years old), it turned out that the more portable electronic devices, such as mobile phones, teenagers owned the more they took their dog out for walks! Obviously, we can only speculate on why, but it isn't unreasonable to think that a dog walk feels both nicer and safer with a smartphone in your pocket.

Teenagers living near 'walkable' green areas of the city also went out more often with their dog. Research in Sweden has also shown that green areas must be closer than 300 metres from where we live in order for us to visit them regularly. Teenagers who owned a dog got less than five minutes' more medium- to high-intensity exercise per week compared to those who didn't have a dog. So the difference wasn't dramatic. And that's why it wasn't surprising that the body mass index – the relationship between weight and height – didn't differ between the groups.

One way to make a walk more fun for you and your dog is to go out with other dog owners. When you're having fun, you're probably more likely to walk farther and more often. An American research team led by Kristin Schneider studied MeetUp – a social app that enables users to find like-minded people in a neighbourhood – to see whether it contributed to dog owners walking more steps per day than dog owners who only received a monthly email from the American Heart Association with advice on how to increase their physical activity.

The results from step counters showed that both groups went farther than before the trial started. Those who used MeetUp took 500 more steps on average than those who only received information and advice. This was a relatively small difference that wasn't statistically significant, but the people who used MeetUp at least had more fun during their walks than they did before.

And after the six-month-long trial ended, the participants continued using MeetUp spontaneously – a good sign, in other words. This study shows that it's not always enough just to read information about what is good for us. To have a lasting change, we must have fun as well, and this is where social media like Facebook, MeetUp and HappyTail can help us find like-minded people to keep us company on our dog walks.

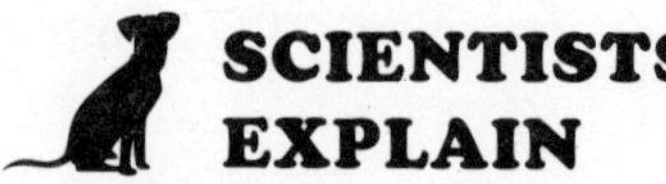

Healthy dog walks

- Dogs' exercise needs vary according to the breed that you have but every dog should have at least one walk a day, preferably two.
- The better the bond between owner and dog, the more likely it is that the dog will be taken for regular walks.
- Pensioners and teenagers who are dog owners are somewhat more physically active than non-dog owners.
- The dog walk will last longer and happen more often if the owner has fun during the walk, for example in the company of other dog-friendly people.

3

Communicating with your dog

DOGS' ABILITY TO understand us is truly amazing. They are exceptionally attentive to our desires, and they understand both our verbal commands and our body language. In this chapter, you'll read about the latest scientific findings on the significance of eye contact and how the dog really interprets our gestures. You'll also read what it is that motivates your dog to obey you.

The attentive dog

You may already have heard the idea that your body language and tone of voice convey far more of your message than what you're actually saying. But we need to take that idea with a pinch of salt because it definitely doesn't apply to all communication. It originates from an experiment performed by the American psychologist Albert Mehrabian in the 1950s.

In the experiment a speaker was instructed to express emotions with words that were vastly different from what their body language and tone of voice implied. In this situation, when there were obvious lies coming out of the person's mouth, the recipient of the message trusted the speaker's body language far more than what was actually said. However, to go from here and conclude that most communication is non-verbal is bold, to say the least. Maybe it works better for communication between dog and human? More recent research shows that dogs have an exceptional understanding of our body language.

'Children don't do as you say; they do as you do' is a common expression that these days has received its own equivalent in dog training: the 'Do as I do' (DAID) method. The method starts from the thesis that the dog wants to imitate what the human does and from this basis it's possible to develop desired behaviours in the dog.

Two Hungarian researchers, Claudia Fugazza and Ádam Miklósi, evaluated (in an article in *Applied Animal Behaviour Science*) the effectiveness of this method compared to traditional clicker training, in which one uses a clicker to form the dog's spontaneous behaviours in a desired direction. A reward in the shape of a dog treat after a click reinforces the message when the dog does the right thing. In this way, the dog can learn to do gradually more difficult tasks according to a plan, through trial and error.

The DAID method takes into account the dogs' desire to mirror what humans do. The trainer shows an action first and then the dog repeats the trainer's movements on the command 'Do it!' Once again, the dog receives a reward when it does the right thing.

The Hungarian researchers tested the effectiveness of each method with 38 dogs: each dog had to, first, fully open a cabinet door that was already slightly ajar and, second, lift both its front paws in the air from a standing position. None of the dogs had performed similar tasks before, but it was clear that the DAID method was more effective because more of the dogs trained using this method managed to repeat the tasks five times within 30 minutes. It also took the dogs less time to perform the two tasks correctly with the DAID method.

The dogs in the 'clicker group' and 'DAID group' that passed the tests later participated in a follow-up experiment. The dogs had to connect the tasks with commands they'd never heard before. Then, after a gap of 24 hours, they had to apply their new skills in a different context – outdoors instead of indoors, or indoors instead of outdoors. Dogs that had received clicker training didn't manage to finish their tasks at all in a different context, whereas almost all the dogs that had learned through the DAID method succeeded.

This shows not only that the 'Do as I do' method works very well in dog training but also, more importantly, that the dog can use its skills in other contexts. A French research team led by Charlotte Duranton examined whether dogs also mirror their owners' behaviours in everyday situations without any commands. In the experiment (published in 2016 in the magazine

Animal Behaviour), 36 Mastiff and 36 Shepherd dogs were tested, with equal numbers of female and male dogs in both groups.

In the experiment the unleashed dog and its owner familiarized themselves with a test room for ten minutes. An unknown woman then came into the room and looked only at the owner. The woman had been instructed to walk towards the dog and the owner, and the owner had in turn been instructed to choose between either taking three steps towards the woman, three steps away from the woman, or to stand completely still.

During the whole experiment, the owner looked only at the woman and was completely silent without showing any emotion. The dog's behaviour was filmed throughout the experiment and later carefully analysed. The experiment showed that the dogs coordinated their behaviours with their owners'. As soon as the unknown woman entered the room, the dog stared back and forth between the woman and the owner. The dog was obviously looking for clues on how to behave.

When the owner pulled back, the dog became more hesitant towards the woman and searched for even more contact with the owner to receive support or an indication of how to behave. And when the owner moved towards the unknown woman, the dog became bolder and looked for contact more quickly with her. Female dogs were more inclined than male dogs to search for contact with their owners to get advice in this new situation, and the Mastiffs behaved more independently than Shepherd dogs and looked more often for contact with the unknown woman.

Together, these results show that our dogs do what we do when they're unsure of how to behave and mirror our behaviours even without training. It might be worth doing a little experiment the next time you're out on a walk with your dog and meet a stranger. Can you make your dog walk backwards or forwards towards the stranger, without looking at it or saying anything?

Even if it's considered impolite, we can learn one or two things by eavesdropping on others. But does it also occur to us that dogs also 'eavesdrop' on the conversations we have with other people, and does the dog react in different ways depending on whether we are treated well or badly? Several researchers have tried to answer that question, and most experiments have been connected to situations involving food. The dog was able to gain advantages by receiving more food after it eavesdropped on conversations. And as you read in the previous chapter, there are few things that make dogs as attentive as the opportunity to receive food.

A Japanese research team led by Hitomi Chijiwa performed an ingenious experiment on this theme, where the dogs couldn't expect more food depending on the choices they made – as the following diagram shows. The dog owner tried to open the lid on a transparent jar to reach a roll of tape. If the owner expressly asked someone to help and this person refused, they weren't highly regarded by the dog. However, the dog didn't appear to perceive any difference between someone who helped the owner and someone who did nothing (a neutral person). This experiment shows to what degree dogs are socially competent and that the possibility of food isn't necessarily the drive behind their attitude towards new people.

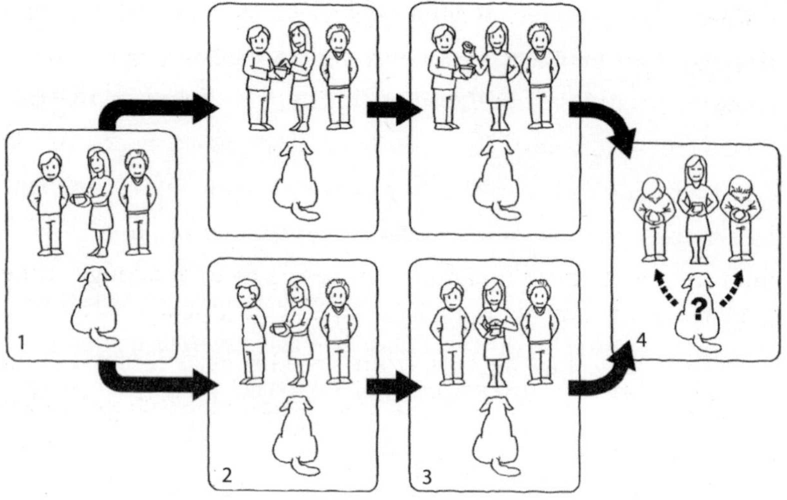

A Japanese research group's experiment revealed that dogs 'eavesdrop', and if someone acts badly towards you as its owner, your dog will subsequently avoid them.

1. The dog owner in the middle has an actor on his right side and a neutral person on the left.

2. The owner tries to open the lid to a jar with a roll of tape inside. She asks for help from the actor, who either helps (top) or refuses and demonstratively turns their back (bottom).

3. The owner only succeeds in getting the tape if the actor helps her.

4. The dog then can choose whether to take food from the actor or from the neutral person, with all three avoiding eye contact with the dog. It turns out that the dog will avoid taking food from the unhelpful person but that there was no difference in the dog's preference for the helpful or the neutral person.

Can it be that your dog even sees nuances in social interactions between people that you don't see yourself? A New Zealand study by Min Hoo Yong and Ted Ruffman showed that dogs do their utmost to understand our behaviours. Dogs watch us for longer when they are unsure how we feel about a new situation. In a similar way, scientists have shown that children who can't interpret emotions in an adult will study a face for a longer time in order to get clues as to what is actually going on.

Dogs also follow signals from humans to a larger extent than signals from other dogs. A Hungarian research group led by Anna Bálint confirmed this through a video experiment showing that dogs avoid objects if another dog shown on a screen stares at the same object. The same dogs were attracted, however, to the object if the screen showed a human staring at that object. It is abundantly clear to us that dogs understand and follow our signals when we point or just look at one of two objects (see also the next section of this chapter on finger pointing). They trust us and know that we wish them well. But we don't know yet why dogs avoid objects that other dogs stare at.

So far in this chapter I've focused on summarizing the research about the conscious and subconscious signals we give out through body language. Body language is important in a dog's world, but, as we all know, we can also train dogs to follow simple commands, such as 'Heel!', 'Stand!', 'Lie down!', 'Drop!', 'Sit!'

and so on. This verbal form of communication can be a good way for you and your dog to just socialize or practise for an obedience competition.

Regardless of aim, using verbal communication in the form of commands that are followed by practice is a good way to stimulate and play with your dog. Sometimes we strengthen our message with hand gestures as we're giving the commands, to tell the dog what to do. But can you make your dog obey your command even when you're at a distance from each other, or even when you're not visible to the dog? And what is it that actually motivates the dog to follow various commands?

A Hungarian research group led by Linda Gerencsér compared how well 30 pet dogs obeyed the two commands 'Sit!' and 'Lie down!' when the owner was half a metre and then 3 metres away. The researchers found that the dogs were noticeably worse at following the commands when the owners were farther away. And there was no difference in the degree of obedience whether the owner was visible to the dog, hidden behind a screen, or outside the room. It was the distance that mattered. Distance from the owner no longer mattered, however, if the dog got a reward from a remote-controlled food dispenser instead of directly from the owner's hand. The food dispenser always stood half a metre away from the dog and wasn't moved around in the room.

How should we interpret these results? Is it that the dog obeys simple commands as long as it's sure there's a reward waiting afterwards, and that the dog obeys better if the owner is close by rather than farther away? It looks as if a working interaction between human and dog is dependent on either a reward in the shape of treats and/or physical closeness between the parties.

Contrary to the Hungarian research, a Japanese research group discovered that dogs were less obedient if the owner was completely or partially concealed. So far, research hasn't reached a conclusive answer to what motivates the dog to obey commands. You can test it yourself at home: how well does your dog obey different commands when none of the parts in the trinity – proximity, eye contact and reward – are present?

In the sport of dog agility, the handler directs the dog to run through an obstacle course as fast and as accurately as possible. This demands that the dog and the handler attend to each other's signals for the interaction to succeed. Even if it's supposed to be fun for both the dog and the handler, there's an obvious chance that both parties become so excited by the competitive moment that stressors come into play. It may be that the dog becomes anxious as well if the handler is stressed during the contest. Communication between handler and dog should be eased if both 'get started' at the same time. An uninterested dog and an engaged handler will probably not lead to any great results on the course.

A recently published American study by Alicia Philips Buttner and colleagues showed that the stress levels in a dog and handler matched each other both before and after a contest in agility. And this result had nothing to do with whether the handler was confirmative (expressing praise) or non-confirmative (punitive) towards the dog after the competition. Saliva tests showed that the amount of cortisol, the stress hormone, increased in the dog as a result of the handler's stress during the competition. This is actually one of the first times ever that researchers have shown a synchronization in hormone levels between two species. In the section on eye contact later in this chapter you will read that even the levels of the happiness hormone between owner and dog can match each other.

The more researchers investigate the physiological reactions of dogs and humans when they interact, the more we realize what a unique position the dog has in our lives. 'Man's best friend' is indeed quite apposite!

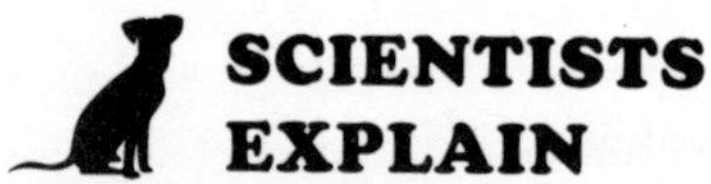

The attentive dog

- Dogs are exceptionally attuned to human body language.
- The DAID ('Do as I do') method seems to be a quicker and more efficient way to teach dogs various exercises than the traditional clicker method.
- Even without training, dogs mirror our behaviours – for example, they will follow our cues when we meet an unfamiliar person when we're out walking our dog.
- Dogs 'eavesdrop' and will know when someone behaves badly towards you as their owner, and they prefer helpful to unhelpful people.

- Dogs obey commands better when their handler is close by and has eye contact with them, and when you reward them with something like a dog treat afterwards.
- Stress levels in dog and handler match each other when they compete in an agility trial.

Finger pointing

The rule that it's not polite to point your finger does not apply in dog research. Scientists point fingers, hands, arms and even legs. The most common test used to find out whether the dog understands what we mean when we give point signals is when a researcher gives a short signal through pointing at one out of two objects in the dog's vicinity. The dog is then allowed to choose freely. If it follows the researcher's pointing motion, it is often rewarded. Dogs excel at this type of game and their ability is comparable to that of a two-year-old child. The dog seems to understand our intentions when we point, despite only using body language. There have been many exciting articles published recently that try to explain in detail how dogs think when they follow our pointing.

In an article published in 2015 in the *Journal of Comparative Psychology*, Tibor Tauzin and colleagues from Hungary investigated whether dogs interpret our pointing motions as assigning a direction or as an instruction to investigate a specific object. To answer this question, the researchers performed a simple but ingenious experiment with the help of 59 different dogs from 13 different breeds. A soft toy kangaroo was placed 75 centimetres to the left and a soft toy pig 75 centimetres to the right of one of the researchers. When the dog entered the room with its owner, the researcher called the dog by name – 'Look, Molly!' for example – and then made eye contact before pointing at one of the stuffed toys for a second. After that, he bent down and picked up both soft toys and then turned round completely. With his back to the dog, he then put the toys (which had switched places) on the floor again and let his arms hang limply by his side. The owner then let the dog go, saying 'Fetch!' without pointing. This process was repeated several times with different soft toys, and with the dog coming from the other side of the room.

The experiment showed clearly that dogs will go to the spot and not to the soft toy the researcher has pointed at. The researchers therefore concluded that dogs interpret our pointing

1. The researcher puts a soft toy kangaroo on his right and a soft toy pig on his left.

2. The researcher calls the dog. When they have eye contact, he points at the toy pig.

motion as an indication of direction rather than an indication of an interesting object.

The experiment was then repeated, but with a twist. This time the researcher wore sunglasses and looked down at the floor the whole time. He didn't speak to the dog either. He only clapped his hands to gain the dog's attention. Other than that, the researcher repeated the first experiment. This time the dogs showed no preference: the spot they went to was entirely random. So it seems that the dog needs a triggering signal – eye contact, for example, or its name called – in order to understand our intentions.

These dogs have probably learned during their upbringing that they're expected to do something when their owner looks for eye contact and calls their name – and maybe that a reward for this behaviour will also be forthcoming.

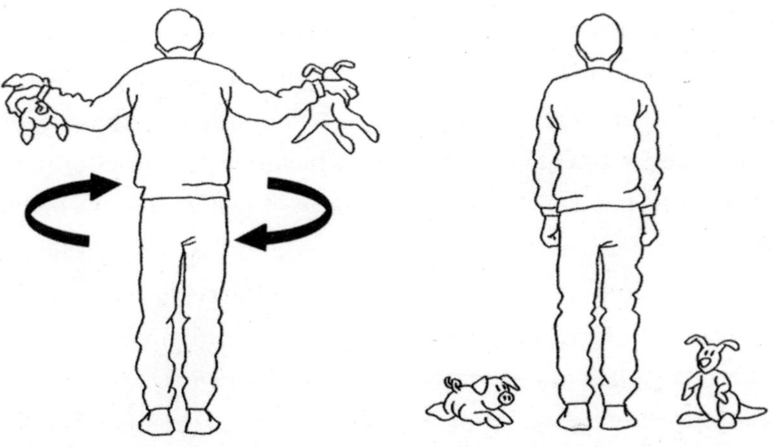

3. The researcher then picks up the soft toys and turns round completely.

4. The researcher with his back turned puts down the soft toys. The owner releases the dog, saying: 'Fetch!' (The dog then went to the kangaroo.)

The researcher Richard Moore and his colleagues asked themselves whether the statement of intent in the form of tone of voice, eye contact and body language determines whether dogs will understand our intentions. 'Now we're going to play' said with a joyful and engaged voice ought to make a dog more enthusiastic about a future challenge, at least compared to its owner saying 'Want to play?' without engagement or looking the dog in the eye. They also wondered whether children are better than dogs at understanding what adults want if they're put in front of the same challenges as dogs. To answer the question, the researchers let a total of 61 children who were just over two years old and 70 pet dogs participate in a fun experiment of hide-and-seek.

The researcher put on either side of her a plastic bucket attached to a rope, which she could pull. In one of the buckets was either a toy for the children or a treat for the dogs. The participants were able to familiarize themselves with the device so they understood that either a toy or a treat awaited if they chose the right bucket. After that, the experiment started and the researcher showed different degrees of engagement, either making eye contact, smiling and saying happily, 'And now ...' while pulling the rope attached to one of the buckets, or looking at the floor all the time and saying in a bored tone, 'And now ...' while pulling the rope.

Each of these hide-and-seek games varied: either the researcher pulled one of the ropes in a very obvious way to show that they were about to play a game, or she 'accidentally' pulled one of the buckets up. In the latter case, the researcher put her hands to her mouth and said with a surprised look, 'Oops!' The researchers investigated later how often the children and the dogs chose correctly in different situations. It turns out that

When we are clear in our intentions – first through eye contact and then pointing – the pointing movement works exceedingly well to indicate in which direction the dog should move. But if the expected signal doesn't come, the dog becomes confused instead. In this experiment the dog focused on maintaining eye contact with the engaged test leader and completely forgot about which bucket moved (where a treat awaited).

dogs and two-year-olds react entirely different to the games. The children chose more often the correct bucket when the researcher clearly pulled the rope, but when she 'accidentally' pulled it, they chose buckets at random. And it didn't matter for the result whether the researcher was engaged or uninspired. The dogs, however, chose the correct bucket more often when the researcher didn't look for eye contact and spoke with an uninterested voice. And it didn't make any difference to the result whether the researcher pulled the rope 'accidentally' or with a clear intention.

Moore and his colleagues think the dogs had so much focus on maintaining eye contact with the engaged researcher that they forgot to look at the buckets. The children, on the other hand, understood whether something is done intentionally or not and therefore ignored the researcher's 'accidentally' pulling one of the ropes. In a follow-up experiment, the engaged researcher pointed at the correct bucket with her index finger for the dogs, while looking back and forth between dog and bucket. That's when the penny dropped and the dogs chose the right bucket more often than at random.

It may be that the dog waited for the right signal to begin the game and didn't understand that the bucket they saw being lifted out of the corner of their eye had something to do with the hide-and-seek. When we are clear in our intentions (eye contact, happy voice), the pointing works well to indicate what direction the dog should go in. But if the expected signal doesn't come when we have the dog's full attention, the dog is confused and awaits further instructions instead.

What happens if we trick the dog with our pointing? Do we lose the dog's confidence and will it not trust us any more? A Japanese research team led by Akiko Takaoka did a simple experiment. In the test room, a researcher hid a dog's favourite treat in one of two opaque plastic containers. When the dog entered the room, the researcher first pointed at the plastic box containing the treat. For the next attempt, the dog watched as the researcher put the treat in a container but then pointed at the wrong one. Finally, the researcher pointed once more at the correct box but the dog didn't know ahead which of the containers had the treat.

A total of 34 dogs from 11 different breeds did this confidence experiment. The dogs followed the researcher's pointing in 58 per cent of the cases at the first attempt, compared to 13 per cent of the cases at the third. It also took longer for the dog to make a choice at all in the final attempt. The researcher obviously lost the dog's trust by pointing at the wrong plastic box in between.

Did the dogs lose trust in other people as well, or was it just in the researcher? To answer this question, the Japanese research team repeated the experiment but this time they replaced the first test leader with a new person after the second attempt. Maybe the dogs would trust this new person more?

The dogs definitely followed the pointing movements more often when there was a new test leader at the third attempt compared to having the same person present in all three attempts (in 39 per cent of the cases compared to 13 per cent previously). In practice, these results mean that dogs don't seem to generalize. Faith between you and your dog can take a long time to build but it can also be lost very quickly. Researchers want to move on and study whether the lost trust for the deceitful person only applies to pointing, or whether the dog becomes more distrustful in other situations as well.

A dog's early life is of great importance in explaining how well it understands various pointing movements. Several research groups have shown this by comparing pet dogs and kennel dogs. That dogs accept humans as their social partners seems to be inborn, which obviously makes it easier when breeding desired behaviours, such as decreased aggressiveness and fear of new situations (see Chapter 6). Dogs don't seem to automatically understand what we mean by pointing, however, but this is something they can be trained to learn. And dogs definitely have an incentive to learn because we pat, play and give them treats when they obey our ritualized pointing signals.

SCIENTISTS EXPLAIN

Finger pointing

- Dogs are better than the human's closest relative, the chimpanzee, at understanding and following pointing movements.
- Dogs interpret pointing as an indication of the direction in which they should go.
- Eye contact with your dog, combined with calling out its name before pointing, increases the chance of the dog understanding what you mean.
- If you deliberately mislead the dog by pointing in a direction where no reward awaits, you will lose the dog's trust to some degree.
- The dog's early life and how much training it receives will determine how well it follows pointing movements.

Eye contact

Our desire always to try to understand our surroundings manifests itself in many different ways. One is that we almost reflexively try to follow other people's gaze. If you stand in the crowd at a sports event or a concert and you notice that the person next to you is staring in a different direction to everyone else, don't you look there too, just to see what's going on? That dogs search for and follow our gaze during training is well known, especially when there's a treat waiting after good behaviour.

During puppy training we encourage the dog to listen to its name and search for eye contact, and after that we start the actual exercise. Sometimes we strive to get the dog to follow our gaze if there's something we want them to be alerted to, but we might not be fully aware of the subconscious signals we send. We might, for example, point our body in a certain direction or point with the finger. It is difficult to determine whether the dog follows just our gaze or the other signals that we give. In everyday situations, we look here and there, and the dog learns after a while that it's seldom worth following our gaze.

A research group led by Lisa Wallis recently investigated in detail whether a dog's age and past training affect how much it follows our gaze when we look somewhere far away. To assist them, the researchers had 145 Border Collies between the

Younger and older dogs follow our gaze more often than middle-aged dogs. Even dogs with little or no training generally follow our gaze more than those with a long history of training. Trained middle-aged dogs are better at controlling their impulses and therefore will focus more on our faces.

ages of 6 months to almost 14 years. The researchers trained the dogs to focus on their faces and when they did it correctly, they received a click with the clicker followed by a piece of sausage. When the experiment started, each Collie sat straight in front of the researcher, who called the dog's name and then said, 'Look!'

The researcher gave a surprised look when the dog looked her in the face, and then turned her head and looked at the door a couple of metres away. Within 10 seconds about 40 per cent of the dogs followed the researcher's gaze to the door. Younger and older dogs followed the researcher's gaze more often than middle-aged dogs, and the researchers believe this is because middle-aged dogs are better at controlling their impulses than exuberant younger and older, more confused dogs. Past training was equally important. Dogs that had undergone long training focused more on the researcher's face and didn't allow themselves to be distracted when she turned her head away.

The study shows conclusively that the dog, just like many other animals – such as monkeys, goats, birds and tortoises(!) – have the ability to follow our gaze, but also that the dog's focus on trying to understand and communicate with us makes it difficult for them to tear their eyes from our faces.

New research shows that eye contact between dog and owner is also a determining factor in strengthening the ties between them. It's similar to the way the close relationship between a mother and her child is strengthened when they look into each other's eyes. The longer they look at each other the more the happiness hormone oxytocin is released in the mother.

In a study published in the renowned journal *Science* in 2015, a Japanese research team led by Miho Nagasawa measured the concentration of oxytocin in the urine of owners and their dogs. The study showed that levels of oxytocin increased in the owners when they stroked, played or talked to their dogs. But the significance of these activities for our happiness was nothing in comparison to the significance of eye contact.

The longer the eye contact lasted, the happier the owners and the dogs became.

Eye contact between domestically raised wolves and their handlers didn't give the same results in either party, however. As dogs and humans have become increasingly attached to each other during the domestication process, eye contact has given the relationship strong positive reinforcement. Just as with the mother and child, a 'happiness loop' develops between owner and dog, and they both look into each other's eyes for longer because both simply feel better doing it.

A prerequisite for this loop not to be broken is that the eye contact lingers when the concentration of oxytocin increases. This was confirmed when the Japanese researchers in a follow-up test gave nasal spray with either oxytocin or cooking salt solution (the control) to the dogs. The dogs that received nasal spray with oxytocin looked for more eye contact with their owners than the dogs that had received the salt solution. It was a so-called blind test where the owners had no idea which dogs had received what spray. Because the dogs searched for more direct eye contact, the levels of oxytocin in turn increased in the owners.

Initial first eye contact between dog and owner is usually followed by the owner bending down to stroke or cuddle the dog. For this experiment, however, the owners were instructed not to talk to or touch their dogs. This could have been the cause of the concentration of oxytocin not increasing *further* in the dogs after the nasal spray had been given. The 'happiness loop' was broken because the owners' odd behaviour did not fully solidify the friendship bond.

Researchers can't yet explain why only female dogs and not male dogs searched for more eye contact after an oxytocin spray.

They've also had similar results on humans where only women react in this way. But one thing is abundantly clear: eye contact plays a decisive role in the 'happiness loop' between owner and dog. We may wonder, then, how it works for guide dogs that don't get eye contact with their blind owner. Do they become unhappy if they are unable to confirm and strengthen friendship bonds with their owners through eye contact?

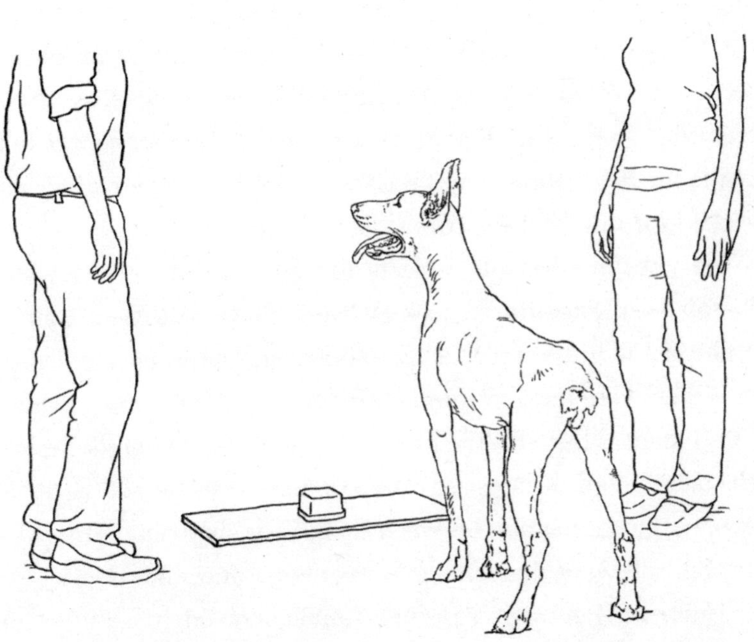

'The impossible task' is often used in behavioural science to study how a dog seeks help from the human and in what way.

The 'impossible task' is often used in behavioural science to study how dogs communicate with humans. First, the dog receives a task it can complete: to reach a treat inside a glass jar without a lid, by turning the jar with the help of their paw or nose. In the next step, the researcher closes the lid on the jar and the task suddenly becomes impossible to achieve.

Does the dog then seek help from humans and, if so, in what way? An Italian research group led by Anna Scandurra studied behaviour during the impossible task to see whether there were differences between 13 active guide dogs (living at home with their blind owners) and 13 dogs still being trained to become guide dogs (living in kennels).

The unexpected result was that active guide dogs looked for more eye contact during the impossible task than dogs still in training. The guide dogs turned to the researcher to get help while the dogs in training tried to solve the task themselves and looked for minimal eye contact with humans.

This result probably reflects the fact that the trainee dogs hadn't been encouraged to seek eye contact with their trainers and had had limited contact with humans. The active guide dogs, however, were used to interacting with humans – not just their blind owners but also the owner's relatives and friends. Despite the fact that guide dogs are unable to have eye contact with their owner, the connection between them is in all probability just as strong as it would be with a seeing owner and their dog.

Interesting enough, Florence Gaunet showed, in a study from 2008, that some guide dogs form the habit of licking themselves loudly around the mouth to call for their owner's attention. Even if later studies couldn't show the same thing, it's a fascinating thought that guide dogs have learned to use their owner's sense of hearing rather than vision.

An Italian research group led by Biagio d'Aniello undertook exactly the same test but with dogs working in sea rescue. The Italian coastguard have been using Labrador Retrievers, Golden Retrievers and Newfoundland dogs to rescue people from drowning for 20 years. More than 300 dogs are used all around Italy and they reportedly rescue about 3,000 people each year. In order to work effectively, the sea-rescue dogs must be very attentive to their keepers' commands.

These dogs are therefore trained to seek eye contact so that they can, at a second's notice, jump into the water at the right time. It could be disastrous if they were to jump at the wrong time from boats or helicopters. Therefore it wasn't too surprising that sea-rescue dogs looked for more eye contact than untrained dogs when solving the 'impossible task'. The Italian research groups have in these two studies shown that, through training, we can affect how much various working dogs use eye contact to communicate with their owners. In other words, dogs have an inherent ability to seek eye contact and they can learn to develop this ability further with the correct social training.

In 2015 a Finnish research group led by Heini Törnqvist published a study investigating the significance of a dog's early environment in the amount of interest it shows in humans and dogs in various social situations. Pet dogs and kennel dogs looked at photographs of two people who were turned either away from or towards each other, as well as two dogs that were either turned away from or towards each other.

These four variations of social interactions were shown on a special LCD monitor that could follow a dog's eye movements to measure exactly where the dog fixed its eyes, and how long its gaze stayed on various parts of the images. Pet dogs watched the photographs for longer than kennelled dogs and seemed to be more interested than kennelled dogs overall in trying to interpret social interactions. But there was no difference between pet dogs and kennelled dogs in what they found most interesting: the humans turned towards each other and the dogs turned towards each other. The photograph of two humans touching each other awoke the most interest. The dogs could hardly tear their eyes away from this picture!

In an earlier study by the same Finnish research team, dogs got to see pictures of human and dog faces – one at a time. The dogs were more interested then in the dog faces than the human ones. Maybe the dogs found the social interaction between humans in the study from 2015 more difficult to interpret and they therefore gazed for longer?

In a follow-up experiment, people looked the same photographs that the dogs had been looking at. Just like the dogs, the test subjects looked longest at the photographs showing the dogs and humans turned towards each other, but they found the one with the dogs interacting to be the most interesting. This result applied regardless of whether the subject was a dog expert or not. This study shows with great clarity that dogs, like humans,

Researchers can follow a dog's eye movements with the help of a special monitor to measure exactly where it fixes its eyes when looking at various photographs. The longer its gaze remains, the bigger the green circles. A Finnish study of pet dogs and kennelled dogs showed that a photograph of two people turned towards each other was the most interesting thing out of the four scenarios above. So it seems that dogs spend more time trying to interpret interactions between humans than between dogs.

really are social creatures: both dogs and humans spend the most time on interpreting and trying to understand each other.

Should you seek eye contact with your dog or not? I hope these studies have convinced you that, yes, of course you should! The dog has an inherent need to understand you and there could be no better way for it to do this than by studying your face. With social training the dog becomes even more focused on your face and will be able to quickly act on your next command.

It's more difficult to give general advice on what you should do when you meet an unknown dog. That will depend on the situation. To show your friendly intentions by giving an unknown dog a confirmatory look can't hurt. However, you should obviously not stare threateningly at a dog that shows obvious aggressive behaviours. It's probably better just to slowly walk away.

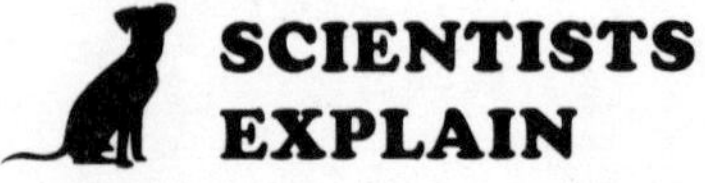

Eye contact

- Direct eye contact between you and your dog makes you both happier. This has been shown by measuring the concentration of the happiness hormone oxytocin in the urine.
- Depending on their type of training, working dogs, such as sea-rescue dogs in Italy, will seek more eye contact than other dogs.
- Some guide dogs for blind people have learned to lick their mouth loudly to attract the attention of their owner.

- Dogs will look at a photograph of two people interacting for longer than one showing two dogs interacting. This is probably because they need more time to try to understand us.
- Dogs follow our gaze even when it doesn't lead to a reward. Well-trained middle-aged dogs don't generally follow our gaze, possibly because they prefer to 'read' our faces and don't like to take their eyes away from us, unlike younger and older dogs, which have more difficulty controlling their impulses.

4
Problem solving

SOMETIMES IT JUST doesn't work out. Sometimes a dog's behaviour becomes too much and creates problems. In this chapter we'll go through some of the most common issues and how you can solve them without risking your dog's safety or serenity. You will read, among other things, about aggressive, frightened and anxious dogs and how we can best help them. Finally, I'll mention how dogs in temporary relocation accommodation manage and how we can make their life easier.

Behavioural problems

It's quite normal for a dog to bark and growl occasionally, but if this behaviour is excessive it prevents the dog from interacting successfully with humans. After all, we are the ones who define what is appropriate for a dog and what is not. Certain fixed and entrenched problem behaviours will obviously endanger a dog's wellbeing and make life difficult for its owner, so we need to find solutions that enable both owners and their dogs to feel better. Plenty of books about raising dogs offer advice and, if they can't help, we can consult a dog psychologist or a behavioural expert.

But what are the most common problems? And what are the main causes of behavioural issues in dogs? The experiences a dog has during its puppyhood until sexual maturity lay the foundation for how it develops and behaves in adulthood (see Chapter 1 on your puppy's social development and Chapter 2 on bonding). A dog that hasn't been socialized at a young age, or that is raised in a home where the connection between owner and dog has broken down, risks developing behavioural issues as an adult.

The key part that its puppyhood plays in an adult dog's behaviour is evident in an Italian study. A research team led by Federica Pirrone wanted to investigate the significance of a dog's breed and upbringing in the development of behaviour problems later in life –specifically, aggressive behaviours towards family members. Pirrone and her colleagues interviewed the owners of 349 dogs bought from small-scale breeders as well as 173 dogs bought from pet shops. All the dogs were more than one year old when their owners were interviewed.

The owners gave information about themselves and their dogs and then made an assessment of whether their dogs displayed any behavioural problems. The results showed that all behavioural problems – such as aggression, compulsive behaviour and separation anxiety – were more common in dogs purchased in a pet shop, as shown in the chart on the following two pages. The researchers concluded that puppies bought in a pet shop are less socialized than puppies coming from ordinary breeders. Even though pet shops in many European countries are no longer allowed to sell puppies, the result still says something about the effect of early experiences on a dog's behaviour as an adult.

Because socialization should be started as early as possible in a puppy's life, it's the breeder's as well as the owner's responsibility to make sure the puppy and the young dog are properly socialized. But the origin of behavioural problems can't just be explained by where the puppy was bought, because it's probable that responsible owners would rather buy their dogs directly from registered breeders rather than pet shops or commercial puppy farms. With the help of advanced statistical methods, Pirrone and her colleagues also took into account the owners' behaviours, background and experiences. For example, did the owners have a dog before, how often and for how long were the dogs allowed out for walks, where did the dog sleep, did they punish the dog for unwanted behaviour, did they go to obedience classes with the dog?

When the owners' behaviours were included in the analysis, the dogs' origins became less important in predicting behavioural problems such as separation anxiety, compulsive disorder and defecating or urinating indoors. In other words, it was the owners' behaviours that were just as important in explaining the dogs' behavioural problems.

This table shows the four most common behavioural problems in dogs in an Italian study and the ten most common behavioural problems in a South Korean study. The percentages show the number of dogs displaying the behaviour. Dashes indicate that the problem was not investigated or declared in the study.

PROBLEM	DEFINITION	ITALY BREEDER 349 DOGS	ITALY PET SHOP 173 DOGS	SOUTH KOREA 174 DOGS
Barking	The dog barks, whines or howls constantly at strangers, traffic, other animals or sudden noises.	–	–	47%
Not housebroken	The dog urinates, defecates or marks its territory indoors.	5%	15%	41%
Aggression	The dog barks, raises its hackles, growls, and attempts to bite its owner, strangers or other animals.	10%	21%	36%
Fear	The dog shows signs of wanting to escape or hide, and trembles or panics when it meets strangers or traffic, hears loud noises or encounters other animals.	–	–	30%

Separation anxiety	The dog shows signs of anxiety such as whining, barking, defecating or becoming destructive when separated from its owners.	17%	30%	28%
Overactive	The dog is in constant motion; it moves quickly, runs and jumps, is restless and disobedient.	–	–	20%
Desire to destroy	The dog tears, chews and destroys things like furniture, electronics, clothes or houseplants.	–	–	16%
Compulsive behaviours	The dog repeatedly shows certain behaviours such as licking itself, chasing its tail or injuring itself or others compulsively.	14%	30%	13%
Sexual problems	The dog attempts to mate with humans, other animals or things like pillows or soft toys.	–	–	7%
Coprophagia	The dog eats the faeces of other dogs or other animals.	–	–	6%

The South Korean researcher Tae-ho Chung and colleagues also wanted to find out whether the relationship between dog and owner can influence whether a dog develops behavioural problems. The researchers asked questions of 174 dog owners with the help of a questionnaire that is often used with behavioural research in dogs – the 'Canine Behavioural Assessment and Research Questionnaire' (C-BARQ). It comprises 24 questions focusing on the dog's background, how well the interaction between owner and dog is working, and possible behavioural problems with the dog. Most of the respondents said that their dogs displayed at least some of the problems described in the table above.

The most common problems, according to the owners, were that their dog barked too much, defecated indoors, was aggressive or frightened, and displayed separation anxiety. Exaggerated barking was top of the list of behavioural problems, particularly in male dogs. Barking and many of the other behavioural problems related to the amount of exercise the dog had and the length of time it was left alone at home.

The risk of the owners experiencing barking as a problem increased if, for example, the dogs went out for only one to three hours per week. Dogs that often went out barked less in general, although the length of each walk did not seem to have an effect in the same way. Dogs taken out for a walk only now and again maybe become stressed from all the stimuli they encounter when they do, and bark more as a consequence. For the walks to become positive stimuli for the dog, 'social exposure' is required – and daily and regular walks strongly decrease the risk of behavioural problems developing or continuing.

Another cause of 'exaggerated' barking was the amount of time the animal spent alone. The risk of owners experiencing barking as a problem increased if the dogs were left alone for more than three hours a day. Dogs left at home for three hours or less barked the least, but if the dogs were left alone at home for extended periods each day (nine to 12 hours), not only did the risk of problems with barking increase but also – for natural reasons – the risk of defecating or urinating indoors. But the main reason for owners to seek help from vets or behavioural scientists was neither barking nor soiling indoors, but aggressive behaviour.

The South Korean researchers couldn't find a connection between aggressive dogs and their sex, age, breed, how long they went out for walks, or how long they stayed alone at home. More studies from other parts of the world and a larger selection of dogs are needed to see if there are any such relationships.

So far, I've been focusing on how behavioural problems can be connected to puppyhood and the significance of the interaction between owner and dog. But research has also shown that several behavioural problems, like aggression between male dogs for example, can be related to the production of the sex hormone testosterone.

In many countries around the world, dogs live a freer life than in some European countries. In the village Puerto Natales in southern Chile, for example, male and female dogs are allowed to roam freely on the village's streets despite having a home where their owner is waiting for them. The free life inexorably leads to the dogs increasing in number, and higher competition between dogs leads to increased stress and aggression between male dogs. One way of getting to grips with these problems is to neuter the male dogs and thus remove or decrease their libido.

The usual procedure when castrating male dogs is that the veterinarian removes the testicles, which produce the sex hormone testosterone. When production of testosterone ceases, not only does the sexual desire disappear but also many unwanted behavioural problems. The neutered dogs become less aggressive, urinate to mark their territory indoors and outdoors less often, don't refuse food as often, are less prone to running away and less stressed.

A cheaper alternative to surgery can be chemical castration, but researchers are still unsure how efficient this method is. A research team from Canada and Chile led by Raphael Vanderstichel performed an experiment in the village of Puerto Natales. As part of the experiment, the researchers were permitted by their owners to neuter 118 male dogs that wandered freely in the village's streets. First they let vets take blood samples to measure the level of testosterone in all the dogs. The blood samples showed that dogs between two and five years old had higher levels of testosterone than younger and older dogs. However, the amount of the sex hormone did not vary with the dog's body weight, body size, or the time of day the blood samples were taken. The researchers returned six months later and divided the dogs into three random groups: one where all the dogs were neutered chemically; one where all the dogs had their testicles removed; and one where none of the dogs were neutered.

The vets took blood samples one hour after sterilization and then four and six months later. The experiment lasted a whole year (six months before and six months after neutering). The level of testosterone in male dogs that had had their testicles removed by vets was almost unmeasurable after four to six months. The operation worked, in other words, as it should. The effect of chemical castration on the level of testosterone was not as conclusive, however. The amount of sex hormone actually increased on the first day, compared to six months earlier.

The scientists couldn't show a significant difference in the amount of testosterone between the control and this test group after four to six months. If there ever was any effect from the chemical castration, it must have lasted for less than four months. With the use of this preparation, the only conclusion to be drawn is that chemical castration doesn't lead to any long-term reduction of sex hormones and behavioural changes.

In the study referred to above, the vets used a needle to inject a liquid, although the preferred method in some countries is to put a chip under the skin which then emits the substance continuously for an extended amount of time. The chip subdues the production of testosterone six weeks after it's been implanted and for six more months. But even with a chip, there's a risk that the levels of testosterone increase at first. After that, the substance is supposed to assist in decreasing the libido. Researchers don't know today if fertility returns to normal after a treatment. Therefore it's not recommended to chemically neuter a male dog if there are plans to use it for breeding later.

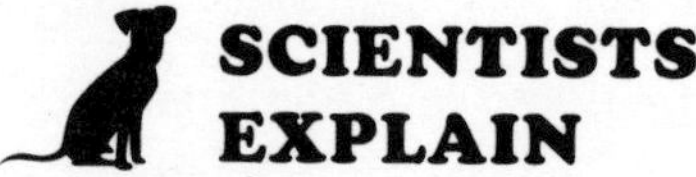

SCIENTISTS EXPLAIN

Behavioural problems

- The dog behaviours we often regard as problematic are excessive barking, aggression towards other animals or people, defecating indoors, becoming frightened for no particular reason, and showing separation anxiety or compulsive behaviour.
- Behavioural problems increase in extent when dogs are left at home alone for long periods each day and if they don't go out on enough walks.
- The dog's origin can explain some behavioural problems. Aggressive behaviour is more common in a dog bought from a pet shop or puppy farm than from a breeder.
- The owners' behaviour, background and experiences can also explain some problematic behaviour in dogs.
- The neutering of male dogs involves repressing the production of the sex hormone testosterone. Surgically removing the testicles is better at achieving this than chemical castration.

Fear, worry and anxiety

Do you know the difference between being scared and being worried? Researchers say that fear lasts a short while and is a response to a specific event that results in the fight-or-flight response. Many dogs become frightened by sudden noises while others are generally scared of new people, situations or objects.

Worry, on the other hand, focuses on the future and doesn't necessarily have to be triggered by a particular threat. If the worry is strong, it creates anxiety, and long-term anxiety affects health negatively. Some dogs experience, for example, strong worry or anxiety about being left alone, which in turn can become a strain on their owner as well.

What's the main reason why dogs become frightened or worried? Are there mainly genetic factors behind it, or is it the environment they were brought up in? And can you alleviate your dog's fear and worry somehow? Two Finnish researchers, Katriina Tiira and Hannes Lohi, interviewed the owners of 3,264 dogs to try to answer these questions. In an article published in *PLoS ONE* in 2015 the researchers focused mainly on the dogs' fear of sudden or loud noises, fear of people, other dogs or new situations, and separation anxiety.

The researchers received answers to their survey from 100 owners of Border Collies, Lagotto Romagnolos, German Shepherds, Salukis, Great Danes and Belgian Shepherds. They found that a puppy's environment during its first three months was a key factor in whether they were afraid or not in adulthood. Puppies that were less socialized became more frightened as adult dogs. In contrast to many other countries, puppies in Finland commonly arrive at their new homes at seven to eight weeks old. This means that the puppy's first experiences derive partly from their mother and partly from their new owners during the first month after their arrival and have a decisive effect on their ability to handle stress later in life (see also Chapter 1 on your puppy's social development).

Sensitivity to sound can be a sign that your dog is stressed, but can you solve the problem? In the same way that psychologists 'prescribe' long, daily walks to depressed people, the study by Tiira and Lohi showed that daily exercise was an effective antidote for sound sensitivity in dogs as well. It wasn't just how many minutes of physical activity per day that had an effect, but also the quality of the walk itself.

Dogs that ran loose were often less afraid of sudden noises than those that were partly or always on a lead during a walk. We don't yet know exactly how exercise counteracts dogs' fear and anxiety, but it's probably due to the increase in serotonin – a hormone that counteracts depression – when dogs move around. The dogs that had daily exercise were usually also alone for shorter periods and had more activities, like obedience courses, with their owners. That's why it's not certain that it's only the exercise in itself that is crucial but it may be a combination of factors that makes some dogs feel more cared for and socialized than others.

The results from the Finnish study also showed that older dogs and female dogs were more sensitive to sounds than younger dogs and male dogs. Dogs more than ten years old, in particular, displayed a strong fear of sudden noises. Lone dogs were also more frightened than dogs from households with several dogs. Finally, it seems that the owners' previous experience of dogs has an effect; the owners' first dog was more likely to have developed a sensitivity to sounds than their second or third dog. Maybe this mirrors the owners' increased experience of training and getting the dogs used to things, or that they are more careful when choosing a breeder when they get a new dog.

When dogs suffer from a long-term illness, it's not inconceivable that they also become stressed, which in turn makes it more difficult for them to regain their health and easier for them to relapse with the same or a new illness. Sandra Nicholson and Joanne Meredith from England used a newly developed method to measure this long-term stress in dogs. As we have seen, we can estimate short-term stress by measuring the amount of the stress hormone cortisol in saliva. The new method measures long-term storage of cortisol in the dog's hair instead, to investigate whether the dog suffers from chronic stress.

The researchers tested 16 healthy dogs and 17 dogs with chronic diseases such as arthritis, chronic bronchitis and congestive heart failure. The results didn't show any particular disparity in the amount of cortisol in the dog hair between the two groups. However, the researchers did discover that the dogs that were left alone for an extended amount of time were more chronically stressed, regardless of whether they were healthy or sick. In some cases, the stress of being left alone by the owners could be alleviated if there were other dogs in the household.

To deal with worry and anxiety in dogs, we first need a reliable way to measure their stress levels. This new method promises good things and we will surely read more about this type of research in the future.

Is there a connection between stressed owners and worried dogs? A Japanese research team led by Naoko Koda wanted to find an answer to this question. They measured the amount of cortisol in the dogs' saliva before and after a visit to a prison. These visiting dogs' task was to make prisoners with mental health problems or intellectual disability more sociable so they could better manage a life of freedom later. To visit prisoners in a usually chaotic environment could become very distressing for the dogs.

But the researchers showed that most dogs had low levels of stress before the visit and even less afterwards. In the few cases where the dogs became stressed by the visit, it was mainly due to the handlers showing clear signs of being stressed by visiting the prisoners. In other words, the dogs mirrored the handlers' behaviours. The handlers also misjudged the dogs' stress in 11 per cent of the cases – that is, the handlers said the dogs' behaviours pointed at them being stressed after the visit, but the cortisol levels showed that the dogs weren't stressed at all.

Maybe the issue was that the handlers experienced increased stress and projected that emotion on to their dogs. The Japanese researchers concluded that the dog handlers had to become better at handling stressful situations and that this in turn could positively affect the dogs' wellbeing.

Separation anxiety is one of the most common behavioural problems in dogs. The stress can manifest itself in different ways, but it's not uncommon that a dog with separation anxiety barks and howls, ruins furniture and equipment, and urinates or defecates indoors when left on its own. In 2015 a group of British researchers led by Christos Karagiannis showed that it was possible to successfully treat separation anxiety in dogs with the same antidepressant medication used to treat humans.

And it wasn't just that these medicines inhibited unwanted behaviours in the short term, but in combination with behaviour therapy it could give long-term positive effects. The therapy included several elements to gradually accustom the dog to being alone when the owners weren't home, and to reward good behaviour when the owners left and returned home. Unfortunately, all medication has side effects; sometimes these can be harmless but often they're negative. In humans, for example, many antidepressants can have a range of unwanted effects such as tiredness and weight gain. We don't know today what side effects antidepressants have on dogs.

However, an article published in 2015 recounted what side effects the medication cortisone could have on dogs. Cortisone is a steroid hormone with anti-inflammatory properties that is often used in the treatment of skin problems or joint swelling.

We know that cortisone has a number of unwanted side effects in humans, but an English research team led by Lorella Notari wanted to investigate if the same applied to dogs.

They compared the behaviours of 44 dogs that received steroid treatment with cortisone and 54 dogs in a control group that received antibiotics or other anti-inflammatory medication. And the dogs' mood was definitely affected. The dogs treated with cortisol were generally nervous, frightened and aggressive, and they reacted strongly when something scared them by, for example, barking persistently. They were also more likely to avoid people and unfamiliar situations. The advice given by the researchers was not to stop treating the dogs with cortisone, since it's a very effective medication, but to inform the dog owners of potential changes in behaviour and how to best tackle them.

Finally in this section, I'd also like to mention a new, even quicker, method to measure dogs' stress levels. If researchers could measure immediate stress – that is, stress in the moment – instead of taking samples and then assessing the stress levels afterwards, a lot would be gained. In that way, we'd be able to see right here and now what causes stress in a dog.

An article by an Italian research team led by Tiziano Travain had the somewhat comical title 'Hot dog: Thermography in the assessment of stress in dogs'. The researchers used a camera that reacts to infrared radiation instead of visible light. In daily speech, it's often called a heat camera and it's usually used, for

A heat camera can reveal whether a dog is stressed or not. The amount of heat in the eyes just inside the tear ducts gives a good image of the dog's body temperature, which we know increases when a dog is stressed. In this photograph the paler area indicates warmer areas and the darker shading indicates colder areas.

example, to detect where heat is escaping from poorly insulated houses.

Equally, one can measure how warm a dog's eyes are just inside the tear ducts, which in turn is an indication of the dog's stress level: the more stressed the dog is, the higher the temperature is. The researchers studied 14 dogs visiting a vet unfamiliar to them, together with their owners. The heat camera was used in the waiting room before the visit, during the routine check with the vet, and finally after the visit when the dogs were sitting in the waiting room again. The results were clear: the eye temperature rose dramatically when the dog was with the vet, and this despite the dog being completely still during the routine check. In other words, the increased body temperature was not the result of the dog being more active: the dog endured the visit calmly and only revealed its discomfort to the heat camera.

This method seemed to work brilliantly in terms of monitoring the dog's immediate stress level, but the problem was that the heat camera itself seemed to release a stress reaction in the dogs. No dog enjoys having a lens up close in its face. At the vet's, they didn't seem to mind too much. They had worse things to worry about then, but in the waiting room the dogs often moved their heads away from the camera. There is room for improvement here to further refine the technique so that measuring the dog's stress level doesn't in itself cause stress.

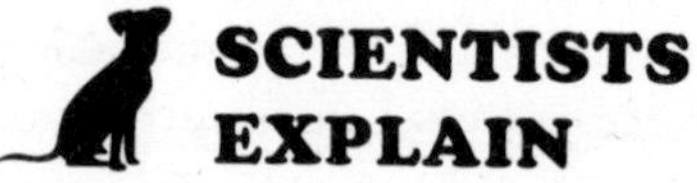

Fear, worry and anxiety

- A puppy's environment and upbringing during its first three months is the biggest factor determining whether it becomes a frightened adult.
- Daily exercise can counteract a dog's fear of sudden noises.
- Older dogs and female dogs are more sensitive to sounds than younger and male dogs.

- Lone dogs are more fearful than dogs in households with several other dogs.
- Dogs left alone at home for long periods each day are likely to experience chronic stress.
- Separation anxiety in dogs can be treated with the same antidepressant medicine that is used for humans. However, we don't know yet what side effects these can produce in the dog.
- Cortisone treatment can lead to behavioural disorders in dogs.
- Measuring the eye's temperature just inside the tear duct with the help of a heat camera can give a good idea of how stressed a dog's is at that moment.

My dog isn't dangerous ...

... it just wants to say hello! Maybe you recognize that excuse, often said breathlessly by the owner of an unleashed dog that approaches you or your dog without warning? There are few things that can create so much irritation between dog owners and between owners and non-owners. Many leashed dogs can feel cornered and take a defensive position when another unleashed, unfamiliar dog approaches in a rush. Not all dogs want to greet others, and a situation can easily get out of hand when one of the dogs attacks. Small children who otherwise love dogs can also become scared when a dog greets them too enthusiastically.

About 10,000 people in Sweden, for example, are injured by dogs every year and need emergency attention at a hospital. In almost half the cases, the cause is dog bites, often as a result of one of the owners trying to break up a dog fight or being bitten during play. It's rarer that a dog bites a human unprovoked. But the number of cases where people have been committed to hospital after dog attacks has increased by 40 per cent in just ten years, from 227 in 2002 to 326 in 2012. More research articles in the past few years have focused on which groups are more vulnerable to dog bites, and how both dog owners and non-owners can help to prevent the risk of dogs attacking.

That people have to seek emergency care in hospitals is twice as common in the USA as in Sweden. In north-west Florida, for example, James Matthias and colleagues showed that more than 400 people per year went to hospital after being attacked by dogs. Children younger than five years are most likely to be victims, and in 90 per cent of the cases it's the family dog or a known dog that has attacked the child at home. Children of school age are also especially vulnerable, and they are just as likely to be bitten by an unknown dog as by the family dog.

Young and older adults aren't bitten as often, and when it happens it's usually when they try to break up fighting dogs. These patterns are not in any way unique to the USA but are repeated in several other developed and developing countries. More than 400 children in Sweden are brought to emergency care each year after dog bites, which usually happen at home or at a friend's house. The background is usually that the child is stroking and hugging the dog.

A dog on a lead can often feel cornered and go into a defensive position when an unknown roaming dog approaches. Not all dogs want to greet other dogs and the situation can easily get out of hand.

Most dogs accept stroking and hugging if they have been socialized since they were puppies, but sometimes the attention may become too intense and cause the dog to feel distressed or threatened. Other usual causes of dog bites are that the dog is protecting its food, its territory or its puppies. Another explanation is that some dogs have distorted behaviour or have been trained to show aggressive behaviour. Most such attacks are avoidable if small children are always supervised in the presence of dogs.

In the UK, information campaigns to inform children in school years 1 to 3 how they should interpret a dog's different signals have been quite successful. The campaigns have had names such as BARK (Be Aware, Responsible and Kind) and 'Prevent-a-Bite'.

Teachers and researchers have realized that dog training for younger ages is also required, when children attend nursery. The reason for this is that, while interacting with dogs, children of nursery age more often misinterpret a dog's signals than children of school age. Are children aged three to five able to learn how to understand the dog's frame of mind after a ten-minute lesson?

Researchers Nelly Lakestani and Morag Donaldson showed 36 children 14 short film clips of different breeds that were friendly, frightened or aggressive. They told the children how they should interpret the dog's mood and how to best read the dog's mood – for example: 'This dog is happy. It is wagging its tail and says hi to the person.' After a short talk and following discussion, the children received a 'test' where they saw other dog breeds displaying friendly, frightened and aggressive behaviours. While the nursery children more easily interpreted the mood in dog breeds they had seen before, they could also understand the behaviours of new breeds. Considering that 31 per cent of all households in Great Britain have dogs and that mainly young children are afflicted by dog bites, it must be said that this information campaign was a success. The children had learned when it was safe or unsafe to approach a dog.

Other than children, women are also in a risk group for dog bites. In Sweden, information from the Swedish Civil Contingencies Agency shows that women are at greater risk of being bitten than men, regardless of age. This might sound contradictory, when studies show that dogs feel more relaxed with women and more watchful with men (see Chapter 2, 'How does your dog feel about you?'). A simple explanation might be that more women than men have dogs or that women in a household socialize more with dogs than men do and therefore also run the risk of being bitten if the dog becomes aggressive.

Most behavioural experts say that almost every dog bite is avoidable as long as you understand the dog's body language and signals. But is it really that simple? Two researchers from England, Carri Westgarth and Francine Watkins, conducted two in-depth interviews with eight women who had been bitten by dogs during the previous five years. They were between 20 and 60 years old, and five of them were dog owners. The commonality between them was that they all had said 'It won't happen to me' before the incident, and after the incident they all said that it was either their own fault or the dog owner's, never the dog's. They all also claimed to have theoretical knowledge about how to recognize aggressive behaviour in dogs before they were bitten.

There were many reasons why the dogs felt it necessary to 'take a bite' and in some instances it happened without warning. In one example a woman kissed a sleeping dog, which then suddenly woke up from its dream and struck; another woman was removing knots from its fur and when the dog felt pain it defended itself; while a third woman went to her neighbour with a newspaper and the bored dog next door attacked.

To pre-empt dog bites in the future, researchers recommend creating an environment where the dogs can't do wrong. Dogs react differently to stimuli, just like humans. Some dogs are triggered when they're woken from deep sleep; others when they spot an unknown dog close to their territory. If we learn which situations could provoke aggression, we can learn how to avoid them completely.

A second recommendation is that once a dog attack is taking place, we should learn how to minimize the risk of serious injury. Information pamphlets for children in England state, for example, that you should 'stand still like a tree' or 'roll yourself into a ball'. A Czech research team studied how people behaved just before they were bitten in the face by a dog, opening up the possibility that we can learn something and avoid some behaviours to prevent attacks. Of the 132 people they studied that were bitten in the face, most of them were children younger than 12 years.

The study showed that behaviours that trigger many dogs are when someone bends over them (76 per cent of all attacks), puts their face close (19 per cent) or stares intently at them (5 per cent). Almost all attacks happened in the dog's own home or garden and the victims knew the dog beforehand. According to the people in the study, the attack came without warning in most cases. Only in 6 per cent of the cases did the dog growl or show its teeth before biting. In more than half of cases there were adults present.

In other words, it's not always enough that a dog owner or parent is in the room to stop an attack, and it's clearly a risky behaviour to bend over a dog. As earlier studies have shown, there was probably not just one reason why the dogs felt so cornered that they couldn't see any alternative but to bite.

In certain situations some dogs may display abnormal, aggressive behaviour and usually their owners are aware of this. But not all dog owners understand how to deal with such dogs. The Italian researcher Paolo Mongillo, with colleagues, came to that conclusion after they had filmed 176 dogs when they were out walking with their owners in the city of Padua in northern Italy. The researchers asked afterwards whether the dog owners wanted to participate in the study and answer questions if and how often their dogs displayed problematic behaviours. Despite knowing about the problems, owners of 'problematic dogs' didn't attempt to avert incidents more often than owners of dogs that behaved well.

'Problematic dogs' also showed less interest in their owner and didn't try to establish any form of contact to get guidance and support for situations that could trigger their aggressive behaviour. That is why I use 'problematic dogs' in quotation marks, because it's more correct to describe their owners as problematic. Dogs are seldom dangerous in themselves, but it's careless owners who create the conditions for dogs to become a danger to others.

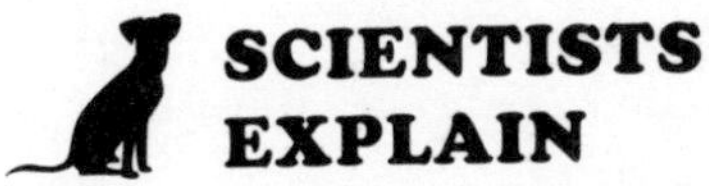

My dog isn't dangerous ...

- Women are at greater risk than men of being bitten by dogs.
- Nursery and primary schoolchildren are more likely to be bitten by dogs than older children and adults.

- In most cases, children are bitten by dogs they already know.
- Children as young as three years old can learn to understand when it's safe and unsafe to approach a dog.
- Dogs can feel cornered when people bend over them and see no other way out than to bite.
- Owners are usually aware that their dogs display abnormal aggressive behaviour in certain situations. It is their responsibility to avoid putting their dog in those situations.
- Most people only need a plaster, but in England alone in 2018 more than 6,000 adults and 1,500 children needed hospital treatment for dog bites. The number of injuries has increased by more than 70 per cent in just ten years.

Homeless dogs

You may have heard of the legend of Arthur the street dog. It all began in 2015 when Arthur, a stray in very poor condition, received a couple of meatballs from the adventure racer Mikael Lindnord during a food break in the Multisport World Championships in Ecuador's jungle. After that, Arthur never left Mikael's side during the tough phases that remained in the Championships. Arthur had made his choice, and today he lives a safe and well-adjusted life with Mikael's family outside Örnsköldsvik in Sweden.

There are many of us whose heart hurts for endangered street dogs around the world. It's therefore becoming more common that we adopt street dogs from countries such as Spain, Greece and Romania, so that they, just like Arthur, can have a chance of a better life. But we must not forget that there are many pet dogs in our own country also in desperate need of a new home.

In the Western world, we know that horrifying numbers of dogs are rescued or left every year with various organizations for relocation: about four million in the USA, half a million in Japan, 140,000 in Canada and 130,000 in the UK. How do the dogs manage during their time in rehoming centres and which dogs have the joy of finding a new home?

A Czech research team led by Jiri Zak wanted to investigate whether there were any patterns explaining why some dogs from rehoming centres were adopted faster than others. Such knowledge is important in order to put in resources to find homes for those 'less wanted' dogs.

The researchers disregarded breed and focused instead on the dogs' age, gender and size. During the course of four years, three rehoming centres in the Czech Republic took in almost 4,000 stray dogs. From these, only 1,500 dogs were returned to their rightful owners after a short time while the others were regarded as abandoned. It probably doesn't surprise anyone that the younger dogs were adopted more quickly than the older ones: dogs more than six years old remained in the home three times longer than dogs less than a year old. Many people probably prefer younger dogs because older dogs are at greater risk of health problems, with the attendant expense of vet's bills. Older dogs are therefore more likely to end their days at the rehoming centres.

Similarly to many other studies on the subject, the Czech research group showed that female dogs are more readily adopted than male dogs. Female dogs are often thought to have a calmer temperament and to be less aggressive than some male dogs. But the Czech researchers also speculated that the reason could be that some dogs' popularity is connected to the fact that humans are attracted to the more unusual. Both female dogs and very large dogs, with a wither height above 65 centimetres, are less common in rehoming centres but they are the dogs that are usually rehomed most quickly. Small dogs with a wither height below 35 cm were also rehomed more quickly than 'normal-sized' dogs.

Most future dog owners probably decide in advance what age, gender and how big a dog they want. But once they visit a rehoming centre, they are often charmed by the personality of the 'wrong' dog. Dogs that are sociable and seek contact are difficult to resist, and then it doesn't really matter if the dog was not exactly what they had thought they wanted.

But how do we get the dogs to show their best side to someone who comes to visit the rehoming centre? They should ideally look as good as possible so potential owners can't resist them. We should obviously not deceive future owners, but the chances of social interactions between dog and a possible new owner need to be as good as possible at the first meeting.

The American researcher Alexandra Protopopova and colleagues investigated whether a more structured first meeting between the dog and a possible new owner increases the chances of adoption. Before a meeting with the potential new owner, the researchers therefore found out what favourite toys various dogs had.

The dog and the possible owner initially got to know each other in a small enclosure (7 × 4 metres) outside for two minutes. After that, they played with the favourite toy and each successful 'Fetch!' rewarded the dog with a treat. The researcher showed the procedure first and then let the possible owner take over. When any of them got tired of the game, the researcher put a short lead on the dog and tried to have it lying close to the potential owner by enticing it with treats.

Then the researchers compared how large a proportion of these dogs were adopted in comparison to the control situation where the researchers didn't actively try to engage the dog, and where a box with all sorts of possible toys was standing inside the enclosure. Both in the experiment and in the control situation the researchers answered all questions about the dog's background, but didn't mention anything about its behaviours.

The chance of a dog being adopted increased by two and half times after the more structured meetings, where the dogs had an opportunity to show their best traits. The researchers came to the conclusion that possible new owners firstly assess a dog's appearance and background, but the final decision to adopt depends on the dog's behaviour and social competence when they interact.

Any misgivings that the owners might feel deceived by the way the first meeting was conducted turned out to be false. The survey given to all visitors afterwards showed they didn't find the more structured meeting with the dogs intrusive in any way.

Another way of expediting the matching-up between dog and a presumed new owner is the rehoming centre personality-testing the dogs. This could perhaps increase the chance that the dog's and the owner's temperaments are a good fit. A research team from Australia led by Kate Mornement used a specifically produced protocol called Behavioural Assessment for Rehoming K9s (BARK). The researchers personality-tested dogs at a rehoming centre, then sought out their new owners four months later to see how well the test results corresponded with the dog's personality. If you've read Chapter 1 on personality tests, you could probably guess the answer: not good at all!

It's in the interaction between owner and dog that we have a more true-to-life picture of a dog's personality. The only behaviours that could be predicted from BARK were those that were based on the dog's fears or anxiety, but not aggression or other behavioural problems. About a quarter of the new owners said that their dogs had growled, lunged towards or tried to bite a person during the short time since adoption. And almost 75 per cent said their dogs showed behaviours they'd like to change if it were possible. At the same time, more than half of the owners said they were very happy with their dogs' behaviour, and more than 70 per cent said that the adoption from the rehoming centre had met their expectations. In other words, they probably had a pretty realistic image of what to expect.

Many rehomed dogs may have been badly treated previously and not behave in the way we would like in unfamiliar situations. They also usually experience high stress in their first days at a rehoming centre. The amount of stress hormone cortisol in the blood shows that dogs are very stressed for three or four days. Once the dogs become used to their new situation, their stress levels decrease and after about a week they're down to a normal level again.

What should the staff do for the transition to go as smoothly as possible, to avoid unnecessary additional stress? One way could be to play classical music or allow the dogs to listen to an audiobook (see Chapter 5, 'Music for all'), or to give the dog a massage. Surely it's not inconceivable that dogs appreciate a nice massage to relax, just as we do?

An American research team led by Emily Dudley investigated whether massage could even strengthen the dogs' immune system. The dogs received massage to their head, neck and shoulders for half an hour each day during the first ten days after their arrival at the rehoming centre. The masseur spoke calmly to the dogs and stroked their fur from time to time during the massage. The dogs in the control group lay alone on a blanket for half an hour each day for ten days.

The researchers took blood samples from the dogs on the first and last day to measure whether the massage contributed to decreasing stress and increased resistance to various diseases. They couldn't find any differences in the amount of white blood cells – leukocytes, lymphocytes or neutrophils – after ten days' of massage. The dogs had, however, significantly lower stress levels after each treatment, as well as after ten days. Even if massage doesn't strengthen the immune system, it helps the dogs adjust better to their new, but hopefully temporary, life at the rehoming centre.

Daily massage is probably not part of the standard offering in many rehoming centres, but there are many other tricks to enrich the environment at the home and stimulate the dogs so they receive as good quality of life as possible. The English researchers Jenna Kiddie and Lisa Collins tested a newly produced protocol to see which measures worked best on 200 dogs in 13 rehoming centres. The handlers answered a wide range of questions about how the dogs at the rehoming centre experienced a certain environment and how management contributed positively or negatively to their quality of life. In other words, this wasn't a behavioural study of the dogs themselves; the handlers answered for them instead.

The results showed that the design and environment of the homes didn't matter much. The dogs' life quality increased, however, if they had access to a raised bed and if it was relatively quiet in the rooms. The raised bed not only contributed to creating a more exciting and stimulating room, but it was also important in giving the dogs the opportunity to see what was happening around them. It's probably just as frustrating for dogs as it is for humans to be able to hear but not see what's happening in their immediate surroundings.

Various forms of physical activity were also a determining factor in the dogs' wellbeing, especially if each activity lasted longer than half an hour and involved more uncommon methods such as swimming. It was definitely better for the dogs to go out once a day, but stay out longer, than several times a day but for a shorter time. The researchers believe that dogs in rehoming centres become too excited if they go out several times a day. The situation could possibly become chaotic when many excited dogs are going out at the same time.

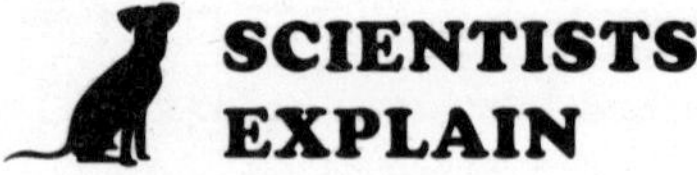

Homeless dogs

- Dogs less than one year old are adopted sooner from rehoming centres than older dogs and male dogs.
- Small dogs under 35 centimetres high and really big dogs over 65 centimetres high are adopted faster than middle-sized and large dogs.
- A 'structured' first meeting between dog and potential new owner significantly increases the chances of adoption. This meeting involves playing with the dog's favourite toy and letting the dog lie close to the potential new owner.

- Personality tests that rehoming centres perform don't give a full picture of how a dog will behave once it has a new home.
- The stress levels in newly brought-in dogs decrease after massage. However, massaged dogs aren't more resistant to diseases.
- A raised bed and longer exercise each day may help to increase the dog's quality of life in a rehoming centre.

5
Your dog's health

THIS CHAPTER IS about all the factors that influence your dog's health and life expectancy. Just like humans, dogs are more prone to various diseases as they get older, and both dogs and humans are, to a large extent, also affected by the so-called 'social diseases' that result from being overweight. Walking more and eating less – and consuming healthier food – can help to rectify the problem in both species. This chapter also discusses some of the diseases that can be spread through dogs' faeces and how you can guard against them.

Eternal youth?

The dream of eternal life! Imagine if we and our dogs could live a longer life together – and not just a longer life, but a life free from the diseases and ailments that often come with old age. We are more successful than ever at treating age-related illnesses such as cancer and heart disease in both dog and human. But wouldn't it be better if we could understand the reasons why we are ageing at all? Then perhaps we could prevent these diseases from ever arising and prolong our lives.

In 2016 a group of American and English researchers led by Kate Creevy published an overview article in the journal *Perspectives in Medicine,* summarizing what researchers know about prolonging dogs' lifespans. A dog lives for 12 years on average, but the expected lifespan varies between different dog breeds: some live for only six years while others can live for up to 18 years.

Whereas most larger mammal species tend to live longer than smaller ones, with domesticated dogs it's somewhat surprisingly the smaller breeds, such as the Chihuahua and Toy Poodle, that on average live longer than the largest breeds, such as the Great Dane and Irish Wolfhound. Researchers have estimated that the expected lifespan decreases by six to 12 months for each kilogram heavier a dog breed is.

We don't know exactly why this is. What we do know, however, is that while the risk of cancer increases dramatically with older age in all dog breeds, with smaller breeds this increased risk happens later in life than with larger breeds. Researchers speculate that it could have something to do with IGF-1, an insulin-like growth hormone, the amount of which varies according to a breed's body size. In laboratory tests with mice they've been able to see a connection between the amount of IGF-1 and life expectancy. But to conclude from that a direct relationship between the growth hormone and life expectancy in dogs is a step too far.

As in humans, many non-fatal ailments arise the older the dogs become. Older dogs often suffer from joint pains, weakened muscles, impaired vision and hearing. Several diseases are specific to certain breeds – for example, heart muscle disease in the Dobermann, spinal disc herniation in the Dachshund, and diabetes in the Miniature Schnauzer – but cancer is the most common cause of death in dogs. One in six dogs dies of cancer, according to the worldwide database VetCompass, which contains information from almost 500 veterinary clinics and on more than two million dogs.

Would dogs in general live longer lives if we one day managed to eradicate cancer? To answer this question, Dan O'Neill and his colleagues conducted advanced computer simulations from the information in VetCompass and another database. Somewhat surprisingly, if we removed cancer as a cause of death, it would make little difference to life expectancy. The researchers got the same result regardless what disease they tested. Preventing diseases in young dogs and maintaining good health for as long as possible is more important for a long life than finding a cure for cancer. The final cause of death is just the straw that breaks the camel's back, so to speak.

The same thing applies to humans: our life expectancy has doubled over the past 180 years, but the main reason for this is the dramatic decrease in child mortality and not that we've become more efficient in treating cancer and other deadly diseases.

Could what I'm describing here have any practical meaning for you as a dog owner? Actually, something that helps dogs live longer is sterilization at a young age. Creevy and her colleagues analysed information from more than 40,000 dogs of many different breeds and ages. They found that after sterilization female dogs live on average 26 per cent longer and male dogs on average 14 per cent longer than they would have otherwise. This is despite their increased risk of dying from different forms of cancer as a result of being neutered. (The only exception to this is a much-decreased risk of mammary tumours in sterilized female dogs.) Neutered dogs have a decreased risk of dying from trauma, infections, vascular diseases and degenerative diseases.

The usual age at which dogs are sterilized varies from country to country. In the UK most dogs are neutered before they reach sexual maturity, usually between six and nine months.

On their birthday all 100-year-olds in the UK receive a telegram from the Queen. To have reached such a distinguished age is certainly something to celebrate! But the achievement is not always straightforward. The American researcher Jessica Every and colleagues suggested that the three main ways to become 100 years old are to 'survive', 'postpone' or just 'avoid' age-related diseases such as cancer.

These 'strategies' apply to dogs as well. Creevy and her colleagues believe so, at least, since the number of dogs dying of cancer between 14 to 18 years of age is much smaller than the number dying of cancer between six to 12 years. Have these older dogs only delayed cancer or have they avoided it completely and can now enjoy their old age? Researchers today can't answer that question, partly because few dogs die of natural causes (Dan O'Neill and colleagues concluded in a British study that 86 per cent of older dogs were put down).

The Dutch researcher Sameh Youssef and colleagues from the Netherlands, Italy, Japan and the USA published an overview article in *Veterinary Pathology* in 2016 in which the results from more than 200 studies of brain diseases in dogs and other animals were summarized. The most common form of age-related dementia in humans is Alzheimer's disease. The brain tissue is gradually destroyed when brain cells atrophy and die, and the early signs include forgetfulness and difficulty in planning and carrying out everyday tasks. After a while, the sense of time, speech and other cognitive functions are lost.

Dogs can also be afflicted by similar changes in brain tissue and impairment of cognitive functions. In dogs, however, it's not called Alzheimer's but Canine Cognitive Dysfunction Syndrome (CCDS). Our dogs are increasingly getting older. In the USA, for example, the number of dogs more than six years old has increased by 6 per cent in just the past two decades and the risk of age-related dementia in dogs has increased to a similar degree.

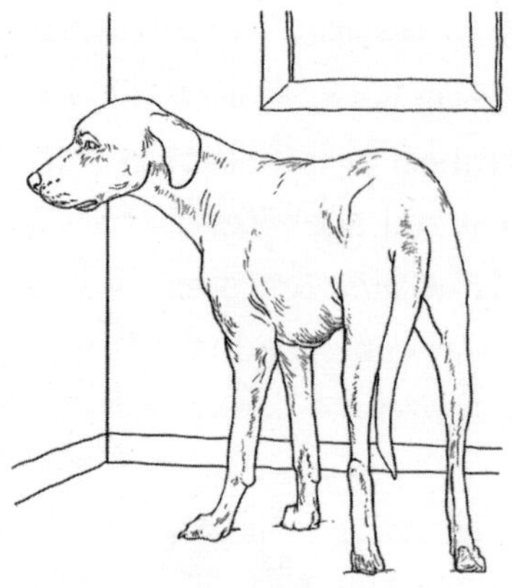

Our dogs are becoming older and the risk of age-related dementia has increased to a similar degree. Canine Cognitive Dysfunction Syndrome (CCDS) is the equivalent of Alzheimer's in humans. Indications of CCDS include the dog no longer recognizing its home environment, forgetting why it entered a room, and staring into thin air.

With a simple test of spatial memory, you can discover CCDS in your dog from a young age. First, you place a dog treat underneath an object, clearly showing the dog where you put it. After this first test, you allow the dog to eat the treat. You wait a while and then hide the treat under the same object placed somewhere else, without the dog seeing you move the object. If some time has elapsed, a dog with CCDS will find it more difficult to remember a presumed reward hidden under the object. You should be concerned if your dog's ability to pass this test gradually diminishes over a period of months or years. On the other hand, it can be difficult to establish what is 'normal' forgetfulness in an older animal.

Dogs with CCDS show a decreased interest in interacting with people and tend to wander back and forth without purpose or direction. Curiously, dogs with CCDS interact more often with their mirror image compared to unaffected dogs of the same age, or to younger dogs. Researchers believe that this is because they no longer recognize their own reflection. One can notice the same behaviour in a human with established Alzheimer's in front of a mirror. Just as with Alzheimer's, there is unfortunately no cure for dogs with CCDS. However, with medication and different kinds of exercises, it's possible to alleviate the symptoms. This is why it's important to identify the disease at an early stage.

SCIENTISTS EXPLAIN

Eternal youth?

- Dogs live on average for 12 years, but their lifespan varies between six to 18 years depending on the breed.
- Smaller dog breeds usually live longer than larger dog breeds.
- Cancer is the most common cause of death in dogs.
- The cancer risk increases after sterilization, but this is countered by the decreased risk of trauma, infections, vascular and degenerative diseases, which means that neutered dogs live longer than unneutered ones.
- Dogs, like humans, can be afflicted by diseases equivalent to what we call Alzheimer's.
- There are no known cures for degenerative diseases today, but the symptoms can be alleviated by medicines and training, especially if they're identified early.

Excess weight and obesity

We must eat or we will perish! Today, the issue seems to be almost the opposite. A combination of too little exercise and too much unhealthy fast food causes us, to put it crudely, to eat ourselves to death. Both dogs and people are afflicted by diabetes, high blood pressure, joint problems and cardiovascular disease. The cause of all these lifestyle diseases is being overweight or extremely overweight, also known as obesity. Several studies show that, in the Western world, between 25 and 60 per cent of our dogs suffer from obesity today.

As an owner, it's easy to feel lost and the questions are many:

- Is my dog overweight?
- How do I help my dog to maintain its correct weight?
- How much food should I give?
- Should my dog eat food scraps?
- And what do I do if my dog is overweight?

In the end, everything boils down to the simple fact that your dog will gain weight if it acquires more energy (in food) than it can get rid of (through exercise). But the picture is more nuanced than that. We know that wolves can go for days without food and that, once they've felled their prey, such as an elk, they can eat several kilos of meat in one sitting. The wolf must have certain physiological adaptations that regulate its sense of feeling full, in order to manage long periods of fasting followed by brief moments of gluttony.

Some dogs display the same behaviour as the wolf. When they are offered food, they devour it almost without chewing. We know today that a strategy for humans to avoid obesity is to eat slowly and chew properly; this helps the digestive system to work more efficiently and we benefit more from all the food nutrients – and we also feel satisfied with less food.

A Japanese study conducted by Nobuyo Ohtani and colleagues recently showed that the same applies to dogs. The researchers filmed 56 dogs from 21 different breeds while they were eating, and from these films they divided the dogs into three groups: 'fast', those that ate fast and gobbled up everything; 'slow', those that ate everything and chewed carefully; and 'picky eaters', those that didn't even finish everything in the bowl. It turned out that the level of their hormone noradrenaline decreased after their meal in the dogs that ate slowly, and even more in those that didn't finish their food. When this happens the ventromedial nucleus in the hypothalamus then receives signals that hunger has been sated. However, the quantity of the hormone *increased* after the meal in those dogs that ate quickly, which stopped the sated hunger signals from reaching the ventromedial nucleus.

Consequently, it seems that these dogs don't 'understand' that they're replete and just continue to gobble. The Japanese researchers then used a device that delivered food to the fast-eating dogs at the same pace it took for the slow dogs to finish their food (little more than four minutes). It turned out then that the quantity of the signal substance decreased after the meal in the same way it did for the dogs that ate slowly.

This shows that it's the speed at which the dog eats that determines whether it feels full or not. But although we can't tell our dogs to eat more slowly or chew more carefully, we can alleviate the problem by providing a bowl that automatically dispenses the food at a slow pace. But probably the best thing to do is to be present when your dog eats, and to give only a small amount of its meal at a time and wait until it's finished before giving more. That way, you avoid the dog gobbling everything up at once.

So it seems some dogs still have the more primitive eating habits that the wolf displays. Some dog breeds are known to be particularly happy eaters and the best-known example is probably the Labrador Retriever. An international research team led by Eleanor Raffan recently succeeded in showing that 23 per cent of all Labradors have a genetic mutation that means they never feel replete, which in turn means that they carry on average two extra kilos of body weight. It's therefore not just their eating behaviour that influences whether they become overweight, but genetic factors too. At the end of the day, though, it's mostly the interaction between the dog and its owner that decides whether a dog becomes obese or not.

Some dog breeds are known for being happy eaters. Certain Labrador Retrievers have a gene mutation that means they never feel replete, which in turn means that they carry on average two extra kilos of body weight.

To find out more about the factors behind dog obesity, researchers from England conducted a survey with a little over 200 dog owners, as shown in the table opposite. The 33 statements were carefully tried out so they would give as reliable and complete a picture as possible about the dogs' eating habits.

The following survey was put to more than 200 dog owners in England. They were asked to respond NEVER, SELDOM, SOMETIMES, OFTEN or ALWAYS to statements from the dog's perspective and NOT TRUE AT ALL, A LITTLE TRUE, MOSTLY TRUE or DEFINITELY TRUE to statements from the owner's perspective.

THE DOG'S FOOD HABITS FROM THE DOG'S PERSPECTIVE	THE DOG'S FOOD HABITS FROM THE OWNER'S PERSPECTIVE
My dog becomes excited when food is available. My dog refuses food when it's not hungry. My dog eats up all its food immediately. My dog is still hungry after a meal. My dog takes its time to finish the food. My dog seems to be hungry all the time.	I am content with my dog's weight. I think my dog should lose weight. My dog is in a very good shape. I'm vigilant about exercising my dog so it remains slim. I change what food I give my dog to control its weight. I am careful with my dog's weight.

(Continued)

My dog is very greedy.

My dog inspects new food before deciding to eat it.

My dog is picky with what it wants to eat.

My dog eats everything.

My dog waits for treats even if its chances of receiving any are slim.

My dog is nearby when I cook or eat food.

My dog eats treats immediately.

I weigh or measure how much food my dog receives.

My dog does not receive food when we humans eat.

My dog is given food scraps from our meal.

My dog is given treats directly at our table.

My dog often receives the same food as we eat.

My dog runs a lot.

My dog plays and chases a lot during our walks.

My dog is often on a lead when we are out for a walk.

My dog is not on a lead when we are out for a walk.

My dog gets an upset stomach from certain food.

My dog has a sensitive stomach.

My dog often gets an upset stomach.

My dog visits the vet regularly for various health issues.

I'm limiting exercise for my dog following advice from the vet.

The results showed that there is no particular difference in food interest between male and female dogs. However, neutered and older dogs were somewhat happier to eat food. When comparing different dog breeds, the one that stood out from the rest as the most food happy was, not surprisingly, the Labrador Retriever. In the debate over dogs' weight there's so far been a strong focus on owners' failure to give their lovelies the right amount of food in combination with too little exercise. This study might somewhat alleviate our bad conscience, because an important factor might be the dog's genetically conditioned interest in eating.

The study also shows that owners of dogs with a greater interest in food are also more careful about keeping within the right 'weight class' for their dogs. Owners of food-happy dogs are less likely to give in to the dog's begging eyes at the table. Rather like the parents of children who are in danger of becoming overweight, dog owners are usually particularly careful about feeding a dog with weight issues. However, food-happy dogs don't generally get more exercise than normal weight dogs. The reason for this is that overweight dogs are usually less mobile and less likely to play. Undertaking more quality training with an overweight dog could therefore be a good way of complementing a careful diet.

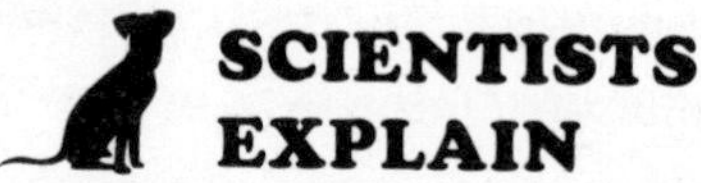

SCIENTISTS EXPLAIN

Excess weight and obesity

- Several studies show that between 25 and 60 per cent of all dogs in the West suffer from obesity.
- Dogs are afflicted by the same social diseases as we are as a result of being overweight.
- Eating slowly and chewing properly contributes to a decreased risk of obesity.
- Give a small amount of food at a time if your dog likes to devour its food. Eating over a longer period makes the dog feel more full, despite eating the same amount as before.
- About a quarter of all Labrador Retrievers carry a genetic mutation that makes them constantly hungry and thus more easily put on weight.
- Owners of dogs that love their food are often more careful about the amount food they're giving them. However, dogs that put on weight easily are not given more exercise than normal weight dogs.

Bacteria, viruses and parasites

It's unpleasant to step in dog poo, but it's worse for your dog. The piles of faeces can contain many infectious bacteria, viruses and parasites, which can make your dog ill.

The diseases mentioned here are only a fraction of ailments that can afflict dogs, and sometimes even humans. It's easy for the most hardened individual to become paranoid when reading information about infectious diseases, but thanks to vaccination programmes and good veterinary care, the risk that your dog will contract a serious illness is small. Dogs in the Western world usually receive excellent care and food with healthy nutrient content.

In the UK it's illegal to leave dog waste in public spaces, particularly places where there are many people, such as playgrounds, pavements, streets and markets. Most dog owners clean up after their dog, but not all. Dog owners can be fined on the spot if they fail to clear up after their dog's mess. In some localities, you can even be fined for forgetting to carry poo bags or 'pooper scoopers' when walking your furry friend. Refusing to pay the penalty can land you in court, where you can be fined up to £1,000.

In 2015 a Canadian research team led by Anya Fiona Smith investigated whether dogs in parks run an increased risk of being infected by *Giardia intestinalis*, a common one-celled parasite which can lead to diarrhoea and weight loss in the dog. The parasite lives on the inner surface of the intestines and is very difficult to kill; it can survive several months in the dog's faeces as long as the environment is damp and cool.

To find out which dogs are mainly afflicted by *Giardia*, the researchers conducted a large survey where they asked almost a thousand dog owners in Calgary about their dog-walking habits. The researchers then took faecal samples from all the dogs in the study. The investigation showed that the risk of infection was clearly connected to their habits. Dogs that walked in parks were often infected, particularly if they ran loose without a lead and were allowed to bathe in ponds. This corresponds to what we know about how the parasite infects new hosts.

The dog gets the parasite by either sniffing at – or eating – an infected dog's faeces or by drinking water containing the parasite. It turned out that fewer than half of the dog owners knew that their pets could get the parasite when let loose in a park. The researchers pointed out, however, that the solution is *not* to keep dogs on a lead all the time – the sociable and physical activity of running freely is much too important for their health. Instead the solution is, according to the researchers, simple and obvious: all dog owners must clean up after their dogs!

The *Giardia* parasite produces minor symptoms in most dogs – and many dogs have the parasite without any symptoms – but other infectious diseases are also spread between dogs through faecal matter. Infections caused by the corona virus, for example, have a short incubation period of one or two days before the dog vomits and has diarrhoea. Puppies in particular risk becoming dehydrated, and even deaths have been reported. But, thankfully, after the infection, the dogs become immune to the virus.

According to some researchers, there is a risk of the *Giardia* parasite spreading from dogs to humans – yet another incentive to clean up after your dog. Diseases and contaminants that

Dog faeces can contain very infectious bacteria, viruses and parasites that risk making your dog ill.

can spread between animals and human are called zoonoses. The best-known zoonotic infection is probably rabies, which is caused by virus *Rabies lyssavirus* and is transmitted through the saliva of infected animals. The virus causes brain inflammation with behaviour disorders as a consequence; infected animals become aggressive and the disease is invariably fatal once symptoms appear. About 60,000 people, mainly in India, China and Africa, die each year from this disease after a bite from an infected street dog. The disease hasn't been seen in dogs in Europe for decades.

The situation is very different in less developed countries. There are an estimated 700 million dogs in the world that roam freely in towns and cities, where they live mainly on our rubbish. These free-ranging dogs also roam the countryside in search of prey, and therefore compete with wild predators. When street dogs interact with wild predators, the risk is great that they will spread diseases to each other. Rabies, canine distemper virus (CDV) and the canine parvovirus are sometimes called 'the big three' diseases and many wild predators die from them after they've been infected by village dogs. The examples are many: African wolves in the Ethiopian Highlands are threatened by rabies, the lions on the Serengeti savannah by canine distemper virus, and wolves in North America by parvovirus.

There are still remnants of the so-called Atlantic Forest in south-eastern Brazil where many threatened animals such as the crab-eating fox, maned wolf and puma still live.

In an article from 2016, a Brazilian research team investigated how much the dogs in the nearby villages carried various infectious diseases. It turned out that almost all of the tested dogs carried parvovirus and a large proportion also had the canine distemper virus and an adenovirus that causes infectious hepatitis. In interviews with the owners of these dogs, it transpired that most of the dogs often ran into the forest and interacted with wild animals. The few wild animals left in the Atlantic Forest thus risk being further decimated by these diseases.

The solution drawn by the researchers is widespread vaccination programmes and neutering campaigns for dogs in the villages that lie closest to the most valuable forest areas. Dogs in Brazilian villages are currently vaccinated only against rabies.

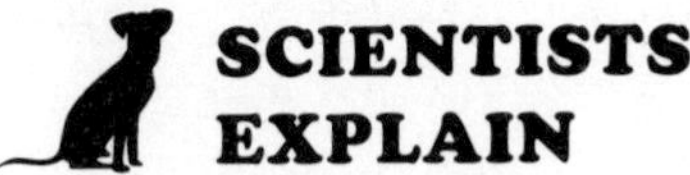

Bacteria, viruses and parasites

- Cleaning up after your dog limits the spread of infection between dogs.
- The corona virus and the parasite *Giardia intestinalis* are examples of contaminants that are spread through a dog's faeces.
- Sicknesses that can spread between animal and human are called zoonoses. Rabies is probably the best-known zoonotic disease and it is spread mainly by free-roaming street dogs. There hasn't been a case of rabies in Europe for decades.
- Vaccination programmes and excellent veterinary care reduce the risk of your dog contracting a serious disease.
- Street dogs that come into contact with wild predators risk spreading diseases such as rabies, canine distemper and parvovirus.
- If you want to know more about preventing health problems and getting your dog vaccinated, visit the British Veterinary Association's or the American Veterinary Medical Association excellent websites.

6

Your dog's senses

THE SENSE OF smell fulfils the same function for dogs as sight does for humans. But do short-nosed dogs have the same sense of smell as long-nosed? You're probably aware that dogs are frightened of loud bangs, but other sounds can make an anxious dog more relaxed – you'll read how that works here! I'll also explain that dogs can be right-pawed or left-pawed, just as people are right-handed or left-handed, and why this might be significant.

The sense of smell

Your dog perceives the world very differently from you. While we humans rely mainly on visual impressions to understand what's happening around us, the dog uses its nose to understand the world. Dogs can detect a single scent molecule in a concentration thousands of times smaller than what people can smell.

This doesn't just help a dog receive an immediate impression of its surroundings, but with the help of its nose it can also 'travel' both back and forth in time. Think about the tracking dog whose sense of smell enables it to follow a missing person's movements from several days earlier, or the avalanche dog that can find a person buried under masses of snow long before the mountain retrieval team can spot them with their eyes. Maybe we can exploit the dog's sharp sense of smell in even more ways. Many large studies have been conducted to evaluate, for example, whether dogs can use their sense of smell to find the early stages of cancer in humans.

How come the dog's sense of smell is so superior to our own? There are several clever adaptations that contribute to the dog's sense of smell: the nose is damp and has a dimpled surface to catch isolated scent molecules; each nostril has a vent on the side where exhaled air comes out, which in turn creates little air whirls that allow only 'new' air to stream into the nose at high speed; the two nostrils work separately from each other so that the dog can smell in stereo, and this helps it to work out the direction different smells are coming from. Furthermore, the dog has more than 200 million smell receptors inside its nose, in comparison to the human's 5 million. And the olfactory bulb in the brain, managing smell impressions, is much larger in dogs than in humans.

A question that has caught researchers' interest is whether dogs rely on their sense of smell in all situations. Could it be that

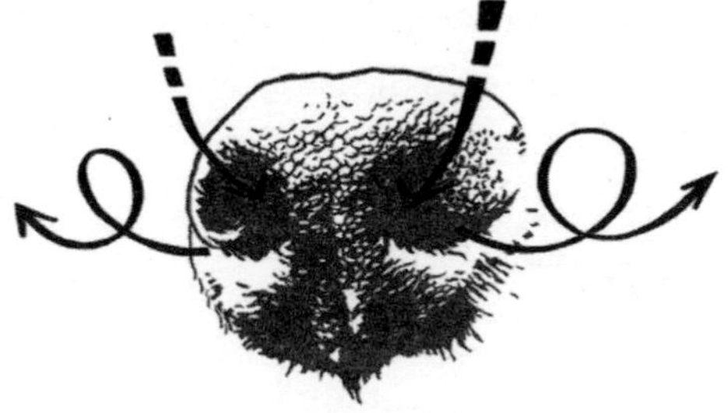

A dog's nose has a vent on each side where exhaled air comes out, which in turn creates little whirls that only allow 'new' air to stream into the nose with high velocity.

their sense of smell is used mainly to search over long distances, and that their vision or prompts from their trainer become more important for finding objects at close range?

It does seem that trained bomb squad dogs rely on smell at all distances. But do untrained pet dogs behave in the same way? A study by a Hungarian research team led by Zita Polgár could give clues to the answer. In an experiment, 30 dogs were given the task of finding their owner – who was concealed under a sheet – at zero, 1, and 3 metres away in three different attempts. At first, all dogs got used to their owner sitting hidden under a sheet. The experiment started once the dog had understood the set-up, but now the dog had to choose between three different people sitting hidden under a sheet in each corner of the room.

When up to a metre away, the dogs found their owner without any problem. At 3 metres, however, the dogs didn't find their owner more often than by chance. They aimed their attention more frequently towards those spots where the owners had been hidden during the practice before the experiment began. It seems that, if dogs don't get an immediate response from their sense of smell, they to a larger extent use past experiences. Maybe it's the interplay between dog and human that's more important for the dog than fully trusting their superior sense of smell?

Do all dogs have an equally good sense of smell? Very few studies have looked at this question. Many of the tasks that police dogs do require a good sense of smell, for example searching for missing people or looking for narcotics. The most commonly used police dogs in the UK and the USA are either German Shepherds or Belgian Shepherds (Malinois). We know that these breeds are especially appropriate because they're easy to train and have a stable temperament. But do they also have a better sense of smell? Or would it perhaps better if the police used Pugs to track missing people?

To find out, an American research team led by Nathaniel Hall compared the sense of smell in German Shepherds with that in Pugs. Short-nosed dog breeds like the Pug are believed to have a worse sense of smell than long-nosed dog breeds such as the Shepherd, but this expectation wasn't supported at all in the study. The ten Pugs outdid the ten Shepherds with ease in the experiment, which asked them to identify which of two buckets filled with sawdust contained a cotton wad doused with extract of anise.

When the concentration of anise in the cotton wad decreased, first from 100 per cent to 10 per cent, and then from 10 per cent to 1 per cent, the Pugs were still much better than Shepherd dogs at finding the right bucket. The Pugs were also easier to train for the experiment than the Shepherds. They understood quickly the purpose of the experiment when treats were offered during the practice session. Researchers don't know today why the Pugs have such a good sense of smell, but we know at least that you shouldn't judge a dog by its fur; just because you have a small nose doesn't mean you have a bad sense of smell!

The smell of sweat can guide us to choose who we want to spend our life with. At least that's the case with mice and humans, where researchers look at so-called MHC – major histocompatibility complex – molecules on the surface of cells. They determine how pleasant we find the smell of another individual. Several studies show that we like smells different from our own. The more different the MHC is from our own, the more attractive we find the intended partner. This is probably a subconscious way of avoiding the negative effects of inbreeding.

It's surprising that the dog with its sensitive nose hasn't featured more often in these types of study. Jennifer Hamilton and Jennifer Vonk conducted a study on the theme 'Do Dogs Prefer Family?', and this showed that dogs were able to recognize their father's scent despite never having met them before. The researchers interpreted this as the dogs using their sense of smell to distinguish close relatives from more distantly related dogs.

Male dogs were also more interested in exploring the scents from distantly related female dogs than from those more closely related to them. These results suggest that smell also plays a decisive part in a dog's choice of partner – at least if the dog has the freedom to choose its partner. Researchers were stunned that the female dogs in the study seemed unable to distinguish between scents from closely related and unrelated dogs. One reason might be that the female dogs weren't on heat when the examination was in progress, and therefore didn't need to show clear preferences. Male dogs, on the other hand, are often sexually interested as soon as they reach sexual maturity. Another explanation could be that free-roaming male dogs move away from 'home' more often and at an earlier stage than female dogs. This is perhaps why female dogs don't have the same need to use their sense of smell to distinguish relatives from others; they recognize each other anyway because they interact every day.

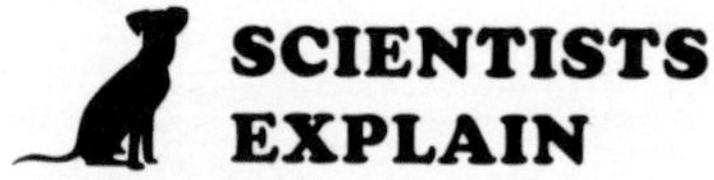

The sense of smell

- The sense of smell fulfils the same function for dogs as sight does for humans. With the help of smell the dog can determine what has happened in the past and what will happen in the near future.
- In blind tests, dogs can recognize their owner's smell, at least at close range.
- It doesn't seem that short-nosed dogs have a worse sense of smell than long-nosed ones: a study of Pugs and Shepherds shows that it could sometimes be the other way around.

- Dogs can sense the smell of their father even if they've never met him before.
- Female dogs are not as skilled, or willing, as male dogs to distinguish between the scents from related and unknown individuals. Researchers don't yet know the reason for this.

Music for all

If you Google 'New Year and dog', you will get quarter of a million hits. At the stroke of midnight, when the rockets are let off and we celebrate the New Year, all dogs frightened of loud bangs suffer tremendously. To alleviate your dog's fear of sudden noises like these, you will find advice on the Internet that includes airport hotels, relaxing pheromones, pure cotton wool in the ears and a protective blanket. You can also cushion or block out the sounds by, for example, playing music or turning on the TV. Just as with humans, sounds can create calm and harmony as well as anxiety and stress with dogs.

Two studies were recently published that investigated to what extent dogs waiting for rehoming became calmer after hearing music and audiobooks. The results were surprising. A total of 31 dogs in a rehoming centre outside Oxford, England, participated in the first study led by researchers Clarissa Brayley and Tamara Montrose. The dogs came in for different reasons: 18 had been brought in by the owners as a result of behaviour issues; five had been removed from their owners because of neglect; and eight had been taken in because they were strays.

When each dog arrived in the rehoming centre, it was housed in a kennel 6 to 8 metres square with a netted fence between the kennels. The dogs had spent an average of 50 days in the home by the time the study was conducted. Even though the dogs were treated well, one could expect, from their disparate and problematic backgrounds, that they would still be anxious. Cramped spaces, few social interactions and a loud noise level in the home probably also added to the dogs experiencing chronic stress. The researchers wanted to find out what types of sound might have a calming influence on the dogs.

The dogs listened randomly to classical music from Beethoven, a variety of pop music, specially produced calming music for dogs ('Through a Dog's Ear'™), and an audiobook of the actor Michael York reading *The Lion, the Witch and the Wardrobe*, the second book in C. S. Lewis's series about Narnia. A tape recorder was placed in the middle of the rehoming centre, between 4 and 12 metres away from the dogs, and it played these sounds at a conversational level. To avoid overstimulating the dogs, the tape was played for two hours on the first day and after a break of two days the next sound was tested.

The researchers recorded the dogs' behaviour every five minutes according to a pre-made list (known as an ethogram): walked around, sat down/stood up, rested/slept, barked, howled/growled/whimpered, or other behaviours. I'm describing the process in detail in case you would like to try this at home. From their knowledge of other similar studies on people, dogs, Asian elephants and gorillas, the researchers expected the dogs to become the most relaxed listening to classical music.

But their expectations didn't come true. To all intents and purposes, the audiobook was superior to all the other sounds. When the dogs listened to *The Lion, the Witch and the Wardrobe,* they lay down and rested or slept considerably more than when they listened to music. They also barked less and didn't wander back and forth in the cage as often. They were simply the most calmed by the audiobook. Classical music contributed to the dogs walking less back and forth but not resting more often. Neither the specially produced calming dog music nor the pop music had any discernible positive effect.

Maybe it was the new experience that had such a hypnotic influence on the dogs – they had never heard an audiobook before. But the researchers also implied that the manner in which the professional actor read the book could have had the calming effect in itself. He pronounces the words clearly and speaks at a calm and steady pace without a hitch. This manner of speaking differs therefore from the conversation of dog keepers, who speak in more staccato bursts. An earlier study on the theme didn't find conversations between keepers having a calming effect on relocation dogs either.

But maybe the positive effect dissipates in time when the dogs become more used to it? A research team in Scotland, led by Amy Bowman, studied this with the help of 50 dogs in a rehoming centre. The dogs were divided into two groups where one half experienced silence – as much as it's possible in a rehoming centre for dogs – for seven days, followed by seven days where they listened each day to a mix of various classical pieces from ten in the morning until half past four in the afternoon. The other half listened to music for seven days, followed by seven days of silence.

A difference from the English study is that the researchers didn't just describe the dogs' behaviours but also measured the amount of the stress hormone cortisol in the saliva as well as variations in pulse – or Heart Rate Variability (HRV). Normally there are some variations between two heartbeats, with sometimes a longer and sometimes a shorter time between beats. But if we strain the body physically or are stressed, the HRV goes down, which basically means that the pauses between heartbeats are of equal length.

A pulse monitor for dogs is therefore a good complement to measuring the amount of cortisol in the saliva to get an indication of whether the dogs are stressed or not. The results from the behavioural studies and HRV (there was no difference in the amount of cortisol) showed that the 300 classical favourites had a calming effect on the dogs, but this positive effect dissipated after just two days. They probably got a little too much of a good thing in listening to music for almost seven hours every day.

For some reason, male dogs responded better to the music than female dogs. There are opportunities here to vary how long and often music should be played, to produce the maximum calming effect on dogs of different genders and backgrounds. Maybe future research will show certain classical composers or audiobook readers to be many dogs' favourites.

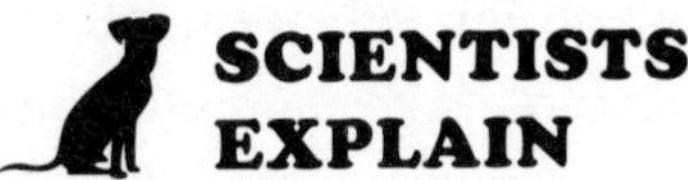

Music for all

- Sudden loud noises from, for example, a thunderclap or New Year's Eve fireworks can be terrifying for many dogs.
- Classical music can have a calming effect on many dogs, but after about two days the positive effects wear off – at least, if dogs listen to it for more than six hours per day.
- The best soothing effect comes from recitation of audiobooks. The dogs barked less and rested more when they listened to audiobooks compared to different forms of music.
- Classical music calms male dogs more than female dogs for some reason.

Right or left?

Are you right- or left-handed? Most people perform complex actions, such as writing a letter or painting, with just their dominant hand. This requires some fine motor skills. Most people are right-handed, but a significant number – about 10 per cent is the figure often mentioned – are naturally left-handed. Many of our tools, such as scissors and can openers, are usually designed only for right-handed people and therefore left-handers often have to learn how to use their right hand for some tasks in order to manage in everyday life.

To be naturally ambidextrous from birth is very unusual, and is found in less than 1 per cent of people. That we have one dominant hand or foot is probably something most people are aware of, but it's less well known that we also have a dominant eye and ear. And many other mammals aside from humans show the same preference for using one side of the body to carry out more complicated tasks. This is something researchers call laterality or side dominance.

Dogs are right- or left-pawed in the same way that we are right- or left-handed. The difference is that, whereas most people are right-handed, dogs may be equally left- or right-pawed. If a dog is given a difficult challenge, it becomes clear that it will always choose the same paw to reach a solution. The most common way of testing whether a dog is right- or left-pawed is to use a hollow, cone-shaped activity ball containing a dog treat, to see which paw the dog uses to stabilize the unruly ball in order to reach the treat.

It's easy to suggest that the dog uses its dominant paw for this task – but is that really the case? In an exciting and somewhat odd comparison of the behaviour of dogs and humans, Deborah Wells and colleagues showed that we have probably assumed this incorrectly all these years. In an experiment using cone-shaped activity balls, 94 people were asked to kneel at a table and use their mouth to take out a small paper ribbon from the ball's opening. To help them stabilize the ball, they could use

Scientists study which paw the dog is using to stabilize the unruly ball to reach the treat.

their left hand, their right hand or both hands. The participants didn't know in advance what the experiment was about.

Of the right-handed subjects 76 per cent used their left hand to stabilize the ball, while 82 per cent of the left-handed used their right hand. When we open a tin can we use our dominant hand for the fine motor skills while we stabilize the can with our other hand, to stop it falling off the worktop. Without thinking, the test subjects probably did just this in this experiment.

The 48 dogs in the experiment did pretty much the same thing, but they lay on the floor when trying to get a dog treat, instead of a paper ribbon, from the ball. To stabilize the ball and reach the treat, 67 per cent of the dogs used either their right or left paw, and the rest used both paws. In both humans and dogs there seems to be a clear preference to use only one hand/paw for the task. It's probably not too far-fetched to reach the conclusion that dogs, in the same way as humans, may use the 'wrong' paw to stabilize the ball.

Several earlier studies have shown that female dogs are more often 'right-pawed', while male dogs are 'left-pawed'. But in the above experiment it turned out to be the other way around:

male dogs used their right paw more often and female dogs used their left. This contradictory result could give indirect support to the idea that the dogs actually use their 'wrong paw' to stabilize objects and their 'right paw' when fine motor skills are needed.

One might think this is only of academic interest – what difference does it make if my dog uses its right or left paw? But it could actually have an unexpected significance when we look into the psyche of the dog. Left-pawed dogs mainly use the right side of their cerebral hemisphere, which controls emotions, while right-pawed dogs more often use the left side of the cerebral hemisphere, which manages more analytical thoughts. The reason is that signals from the senses are cross-connected on their way to the brain. A left-pawed dog may therefore react with stronger emotions to stimuli that leave a right-pawed dog unperturbed. That is why it might not be appropriate to choose left-pawed dogs to, for example, lead dog training where a more stable temperament is required.

Within the research world there are enough studies of laterality that the field has its own dedicated periodical: *Journal of Laterality*. Here one can read about dogs that wag their tail right or left, dogs that use their right or left ear to listen, dogs that first put down their right or left paw when they run, and so on. In 2015 the American researchers William Gough and Betty McGuire published an article that investigated whether dogs mainly lift the left or right hind leg when they urinate.

A total of 264 dogs from two dog shelters in New York participated in the study, and the researchers documented more than 2,000 urinations! In 75 per cent of the cases the dogs lifted one of their hind legs, and in the remaining cases the female dogs squatted and the male dogs leaned forwards. Male dogs lifted their hind legs, considerably more often than the female dogs when they peed, and both genders lifted their hind legs the older they became. None of the dogs in the study were younger than four months, which is the average age when young dogs start to lift their leg to urinate.

However, no side was dominant. The dogs lifted the left with ease and just as often as the right leg. We can only speculate on the reasons for this. Maybe its brain doesn't have to work particularly hard when the dog urinates, and the choice of leg could depend more on whether the bush or the lamppost is on the right or left side of the path. One thing is for certain and that is that the study of laterality is in its infancy and many exciting discoveries will be made in the future. Until then it could be fascinating to study your dog's body language in different situations to find out which side dominates.

Considering that dogs can smell in stereo (see the section above on the sense of smell), it's not particularly surprising that researchers have shown that dogs also display laterality when it comes to the sense of smell. Earlier studies have shown that dogs sniff with the right nostril if it's a scent that causes anxiety, stress or excitement. Once the dog is familiar with the unknown smell and it becomes less frightening, it uses the left nostril instead. Does this also apply regardless of whether it's a dog or a person being the transmitter of the scent?

An Italian research group led by Marcello Siniscalchi showed that this wasn't the case. Dogs use different nostrils depending on whether a smell comes from a frightened human or a dog. In the experiment, test persons watched a horror film for 15 minutes, after which sweat was collected from their armpits with the help of cotton wads. The dogs didn't have to watch the horror. They were instead exposed to the frightening situation of sitting totally isolated in an unfamiliar room for 15 minutes. With the help of cotton wads, the researcher then collected samples of saliva from the mouth and pheromones (scent signals) from glands around the anus and between the pads of the paws. Thirty-one dogs were then filmed sniffing the cotton wads. The dogs used almost exclusively the right nostril to smell the scent taken from anxious dogs while using the left nostril to smell the sweat from frightened people.

Signals for the sense of smell travel across nerve endings from the right nostril directly to the right side of the cerebral hemisphere and from the left nostril directly to the left side of the cerebral hemisphere. The nerve endings never cross on their way, as they do with stimuli from sight or touch. Dogs that used the right nostril to smell the fear from other dogs mainly used the right side of the cerebral hemisphere, which controls fear, aggression, excitement, happiness and so on.

When they smelled sweat from frightened humans, however, the signals went to the left side of the cerebral hemisphere that controls analytical thoughts. It should be pointed out that this characterization of the cerebral hemisphere's functions is a crude simplification, because the left and the right side communicate and coordinate through the corpus callosum. But it still seems reasonable to interpret the results as strong emotions were emitted from those dogs that smelled other dogs' fear. However, it's more difficult to understand why dogs use the more analytical side of the brain when they smell fear in humans. When the dogs in the study smelled sweat from relaxed or happy people, they used both nostrils equally.

Right or left?

- Most dogs are either left- or right-pawed, that is, they use only one paw to solve more complicated tasks.
- Using an activity ball to determine whether your dog is right- or left-pawed could go wrong. Just as with humans, the dog will probably use the 'wrong paw' to stabilize an object and the 'right paw' for fine motor skills.
- When dogs urinate they lift their right leg as often as their left.
- Dogs use their right nostril to 'smell the fear of dogs', while they use their left nostril to smell sweat from frightened people.

7

How dogs originated

IN THIS CHAPTER we're investigating how dogs evolved from the wolf. Humans domesticated the wolf at least 13,000 years ago, which is not long from an evolutionary point of view. How big are the differences between wolves' and dogs' behaviours? And are there also differences in behaviour between different dog breeds? Lastly, we will look more closely at the phenomenon of street dogs around the world. It's estimated that there are 900 million dogs in the world, 80 per cent of which roam free in villages, towns and cities.

The dog and the wolf

The wolf was the first animal that humans domesticated – at least 13,000 years ago, and possibly even thousands of years before that, according to recent research – but it's still a relatively short time period from an evolutionary perspective. The genetic differences between dogs and wolves are so small that taxonomy sees them as the same species: *Canis lupus*. How big, then, are the differences in behaviour between dogs and wolves? And are the behaviours inherited or are they the result of the environment? By studying the wolf's behaviour and domestication, we may be able to understand the dog better.

In Siberia, archaeologists have found bones from doglike creatures that are over 30,000 years old. When the researchers measured the skulls from these creatures, they found greater similarities between extinct types of wolves than with dogs. There are no new fossil findings that date the first dogs that far back in time. Fossils that correspond with today's dog, on the other hand, have been found in the Middle East and in Europe. These findings show that the first dogs can be dated to at least 14,000 years ago and maybe even as far back as 17,000 years ago. Analysis of the wolf's as well as the dog's genome confirms this dating. The researchers have not been able to limit the time interval further, however, but conclude that the modern dog first saw the light of day at some point between 13,000 and 32,000 years ago.

Why can't we have a more exact date than that, with today's modern technology? The main reason is probably that attempts to domesticate the wolf have happened on several different occasions and in different parts of the world. Yet another factor that makes it difficult to determine more exactly when the dog was domesticated is connected to the first dogs cross-bred with wolves.

We see this hybridization even in modern times, for example in the Caucasus region where large herding dogs guard the livestock that wander freely in the mountains. In molecular analysis that Natia Kopaliani and colleagues did in 2014, they found that 13 per cent of the herding dogs and 10 per cent of the wolves in the area in the Caucasus were hybrids between dog and wolf.

Maybe you've heard of the female wolf Ylva, which courted the Swedish elkhound Picko in Värmland, Sweden? Ylva received contraceptive pills to prevent unwanted hybrids being conceived, but was put down a few years later after continuing to show the region's male dogs significant attention.

What happened when the wolf became domesticated? New studies of the genetic material between dogs and wolves give us clues to the answer. In 2013 Erik Axelsson and Kerstin Lindblad-Toh from Uppsala University in Sweden, published, with colleagues, an article in the leading scientific journal *Nature*. They had found that one of the bigger genetic differences between dog and wolf is that dogs have mutations that are better able to break down starch. This supports one of the main hypotheses to describe the origin of the dog, namely that wolves crept around on the outskirts of the first agriculturists' settlements to rummage for food among the domestic waste. The ability to extract nutrients, not just from meat but also from plant material, was a prerequisite for the domestication of the wolf.

But it is not enough just to be able to digest humans' food. The first wolves that sought out humans were also forced to learn how to tolerate and, eventually, appreciate the humans' presence. In 2016 the German researchers Alex Cagan and Torsten Blass showed in an article published in the journal *BMC Evolutionary Biology* that this was actually the case. When they compared sets of genes between 69 dogs and seven wolves, they realized that the main differences between them were connected to factors such as stress, fear and defence. The wolves produced more adrenaline – a hormone that places the body into a state of alarm and determines whether one should fight or flee – than the dogs. The second prerequisite for the wolf's domestication – losing its inherent fear of humans – was achieved.

The first wolves that gave birth to today's dogs wouldn't have consumed our domestic waste on just a few occasions, but would have visited settlements regularly. Because they realized that humans didn't pose a danger, they didn't need to be afraid or show aggressive behaviour. This change in behaviour was a crucial step for the first wolves that became dogs' forebears. They learned more and more to understand humans and their intentions, and therefore began to develop into the social creature the dog is today.

Based at the Wolf Science Center, just outside Vienna in Austria, are the scientists Friederike Range and Zsofia Viranyo, who have studied differences in behaviour between the modern dog and the wolf . They published an overview article in the journal *Frontiers in Psychology* in 2015, where they summarized the conclusions within the field. These showed that researchers have not been able to find any differences between how dogs and wolves work socially, either within the pack or towards humans they know.

Wolf puppies were just as attentive and cooperative as the dog puppies towards the researchers. On the other hand, wolf puppies were more timid towards unfamiliar humans and reacted more strongly to sudden sounds and new objects. So maybe it's not the social ability in itself that differentiates dogs from wolves, but rather the dog's ability to accept both familiar and more or less unfamiliar humans without much tendency to become stressed.

In 2015 the research group at the Wolf Science Center also published an article in the *Proceedings of the Royal Society Series B* that, somewhat surprisingly, showed that wolves were *more* tolerant towards one another during food situations than dogs. The researchers had made side-by-side comparisons of dog–dog and wolf–wolf. The dogs were between 9 and 18 months old and came from five different litters, and the wolves were between 6 and 18 months old and came from six different litters.

The research team had decided beforehand which behaviours would be categorized as dominant or submissive. They had been able to study spontaneous interactions between the animals earlier, to determine which individuals could be categorized as having a higher or lower rank within the pack.

The animals were brought into a test room in pairs where there was food, either raw meat or a large bone, under a wooden box that was lifted when they approached. The wolves of lower rank could without any problem challenge individuals of higher rank, and vice versa. A dog of lower rank never challenged another dog of higher rank, however, and a dog of lower rank that was challenged deferred immediately, without showing any aggressive tendencies.

Earlier studies confirm this image of dogs being less tolerant of each other than wolves. It could also be the case that dogs of lower rank react more strongly in a conflict situation and have learned to retreat rather than challenge. Scientists are putting forward various different explanations of how this difference in behaviour could have emerged – but the truth is that we don't know why wolves are more tolerant in this situation. But the traditional image of the big bad wolf has probably received a setback!

The research team at the Wolf Science Center also asked if the sense of curiosity differed between dogs and wolves. The will to discover their surroundings is crucial for many animals' survival and reproduction. Where can I find food during different seasons? Are escape routes and shelter in close proximity in case a predator attacks? Where are the greatest chances of finding a mate? Neophobia could be said to be the complete opposite of a sense of discovery. An animal that shows neophobia actively avoids an object, a situation or an area it hasn't encountered before. The animal minimizes the risks but at the same time misses the opportunity to learn something new. Could it be that the pet dog that always receives new impressions in everyday life has learned to be less frightened of new objects or situations?

The pet dog also doesn't need to struggle for survival in the same way as the wolf. It lives in a safe environment together with humans, always with a filled-up food bowl and next to no risk of encountering a predator. Maybe that diminishes the dog's sense of wonder? Since the wolf's sense of wonder is directly connected to its survival, maybe this is why the wolf is more careful when encountering new situations? To answer these questions, the researchers introduced 13 dogs and 11 wolves to a total of 38 objects they had never seen before – for example a bicycle, a balloon, a helmet, a teddy bear and so on. The animals got the opportunity to familiarize themselves with the strange objects alone, and then with a familiar companion or pack member.

The sense of discovery was larger with both the dog and the wolf when they had company compared to when they were alone. They probably felt safer and more relaxed with the strange object when they could share the risk with a companion. The biggest sense of discovery the animals had was when they could confront the new object together with a sibling. But the results also showed clear differences between the wolf and the dog. The dogs didn't even try to approach the object in 10 per cent of the cases, while the wolves approached without exception.

The wolves approached the unknown object more slowly and examined it for longer than the dogs did. But they were also more nervous, in particular the older wolves, which ran from the object on several occasions. These results confirm as a whole that the dog has become less curious about unknown objects through the course of evolution. The wolf, on the other hand, showed both a greater sense of discovery and – maybe somewhat paradoxically – greater fear than the dog.

The wolf is a pack animal, and to catch prey as large as an elk, for example, requires good cooperation within the pack. Separate pack members need to control their initial urge to go on the attack, and instead wait for the right opportunity to make a synchronized attack with all the pack members.

Among wolves it is the leader pair that has puppies, while all members of the pack help to raise them. In other words, we expect the wolf to have a high degree of impulse control. Even if the dog isn't a pack animal in the way the wolf is, breeding is expected to have contributed to its less reactionary temperament and its superior ability to act only on a signal from its owners. The dog watches its owner faithfully to get clarity on how to behave next, which obviously requires a certain degree of impulse control.

To understand what differences there are between dogs' and wolves' impulse control, researchers at the Wolf Science Center used two different trials: a detour test and a cylinder test. The detour test involved a reward, in the form of food, being placed on the other side of a netted fence and then studying how the wolves and dogs behaved. The results were contradictory.

The wolf quickly learned to take a detour around the fence to get the reward, while the dog more often stayed behind the fence in the vicinity of the unobtainable food (closest path). The wolf had consequently better control of its initial impulse to stay in the vicinity of the food in this test. In the cylinder test, meanwhile, the dog was better at directly finding the treat that had been placed inside a horizontal transparent cylinder. The wolf tried more often than the dog to place its nose on top of the cylinder (closest path) instead of bending down to grab the treat from one side.

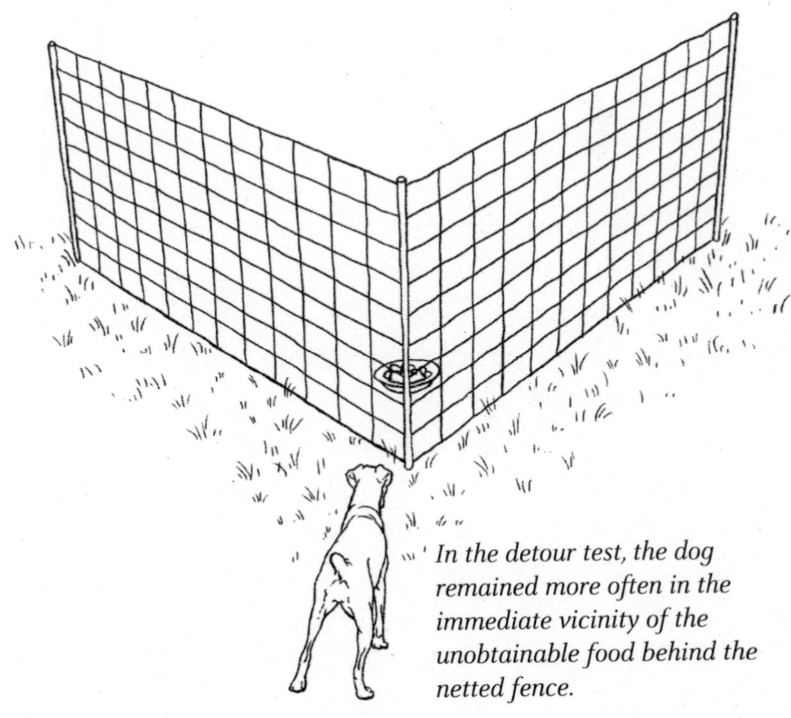

In the detour test, the dog remained more often in the immediate vicinity of the unobtainable food behind the netted fence.

In the cylinder test, the dog was better than the wolf at finding the treat inside a transparent cylinder.

Researchers speculate on the reasons for these results. One theory is that the wolf has a better spatial awareness than the dog: I am here and the reward is there. For me to get the reward, I actually need to take a detour around the fence. Some earlier studies have also shown that the wolf manages maze tests better than the dog, which supports this hypothesis. The dog's success in the cylinder test may be due to the fact that it paid more attention to the human when the treat was placed in the cylinder. Unfortunately, the test wasn't designed in a way that would allow the researcher to measure such differences. We haven't heard the last word on this, and there is room for yet more ingenious experiments.

An experiment conducted by Monique Udell from Oregon, USA, may provide another piece of the puzzle in the matter of impulse control in dogs and wolves, and how it might contribute to their ability to solve problems. To reach a sausage in a transparent plastic box, dogs and the wolves were required to pull a string attached to the lid. The result was that 80 per cent of the wolves – raised by humans since they were two weeks' old – managed to reach the sausage, but only 5 per cent of the dogs managed it. Instead, the dogs spent a long time watching the silent person also in the room.

In a final attempt, the researcher actively encouraged the dogs to try to solve the problem. They then became somewhat better at the task, mainly by spending longer than previously trying to lift the lid. This experiment shows that the more independent wolves may understand spatial relations better than dogs, which rely more on humans to contribute to solving problems.

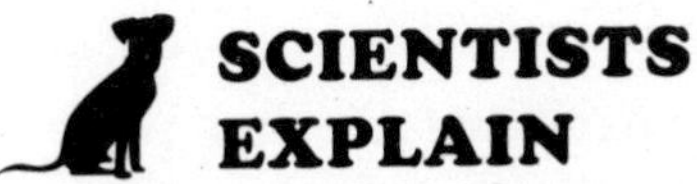

The dog and the wolf

- The wolf and the dog belong to the same species (*Canis lupus*). The dog is believed by most taxonomists to be a subspecies of the wolf (*Canis lupus familiaris*).
- The modern dog saw the light of day for the first time 13,000 to 32,000 years ago. The uncertainty of the dating is due to domestication that happened at different times and places, and because cross-breeding between wolves and dogs is common.
- The dog has mutations that allow it to break down starch better than the wolf can, enabling it to digest nutrients from plants.
- The dog doesn't release as much adrenaline as the wolf and therefore experiences less stress when in the vicinity of a human.

Dog breeds

Short or tall, fat or thin, big or small – the huge variations between different dog breeds are quite remarkable. Just think about the length of an Afghan Hound's nose compared with a Pug's, which is essentially flat, or the size of a Great Dane versus that of a Chihuahua – it's about 50 times heavier and ten times taller. The differences between dog breeds can be so great that they often look as if they are completely different types of animal rather than mere variations within one species.

The enormous variety in the appearance and behaviour of different dog breeds is a result of controlled breeding. Today there are more than 400 dog breeds, each with its own breed type or breed standard, which is a guideline for what a particular breed should look like. Development of selective breeding took off with the first dog shows and kennel clubs in Europe a little over a century ago.

During the twenty-first century the rapid development of techniques for genetic analysis has made it possible for researchers to study how various dog breeds are related. The first of these studies was published in the scientific journal *Science* in 2004. An American research team led by Heidi G. Parker investigated close to 400 dogs from 85 different breeds and found that all but two of the breeds were genetically separate. From genetic analysis they could also see that breeds that were first developed in

Asia and Africa are more ancient – that is, they became separate specific breeds much earlier than the more modern breeds that were developed mainly in Europe.

The research team could distinguish three groups of dog breed in Europe: one that contained Mastiff-like dogs, one that contained sight hounds and herding dogs, and finally the largest group that contained, among others, hunting dogs and pet dogs. The research team conducted an even more sophisticated analysis of more dogs three years later, and the three main groups were confirmed yet again. This time, however, the group with Mastiffs and Shepherd dogs were separated into two sub-groups.

The largest group, the hunting dogs and pet dogs, now also included tracking dogs and spaniels. Our current knowledge about the heritage of 76 different dog breeds is summarized in the diagram on the following pages, and is the result of a large international collaboration that was published in the scientific magazine *Nature* in 2010. Spitzes and the more primitive breeds are most closely related to the wolf and are therefore placed nearest to the wolf in the so-called cladogram.

Modern dog breeds can be divided into 11 distinct groups. The divisions according to genetic factors closely match the classic divisions into the different groups based on appearance and behaviour that the kennel clubs use. Anything else would be a surprise. However, dwarf dogs form a more heterogeneous group of breeds than had previously been believed. The reason for this is that hybridization between a larger dog breed and the dwarf dog (or the dwarf form of a larger dog breed) has occurred on several occasions. It is the same with domestic dogs, where their genetic origin indicates that the breeds we know

Dog breeds

In this simplified cladogram you can see how 76 different dog breeds are related. For each dog breed the genetic composition between six different individuals was investigated.

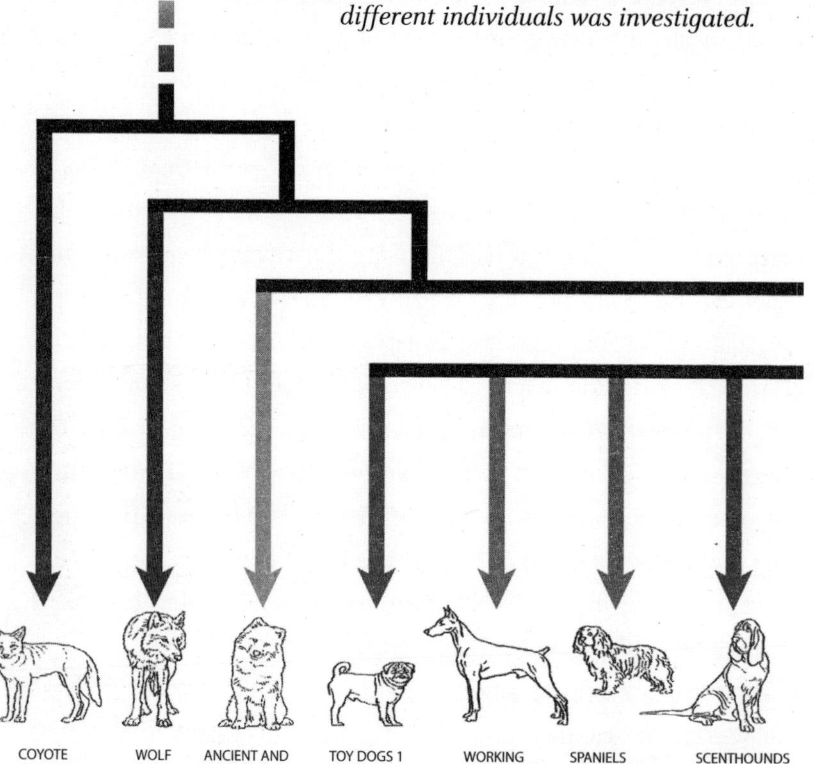

The Coyote has been used as a base in the genetic analysis. Spitzes and primitive dogs from Africa and Asia branched away from the wolf a long time ago. The modern breeds, from Europe, have been created by intentional breeding. That is why the genetic differences between them are small and there are no separate branches in the family.

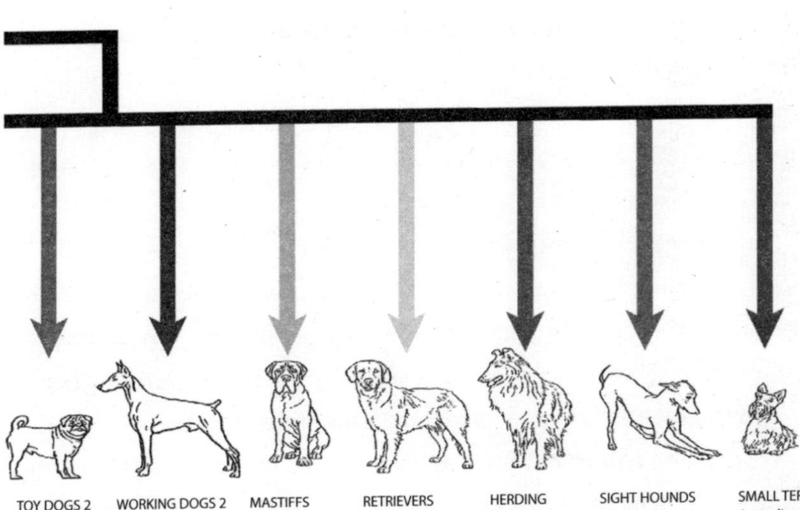

TOY DOGS 2
Chihuahua
Papillon
Pomeranian

WORKING DOGS 2
Doberman
Miniature Schnauzer
Schnauzer
German Sheep Dog
Portuguese Water Dog

MASTIFFS
Boxer
Bulldog
Bullmastiff
French Bulldog
Glen of Imaal Terrier
Mastiff
Miniature Bull Terrier
Staffordshire Bull Terrier
Boston Terrier

RETRIEVERS
Bernese Mountain Dog
Flat-coated Retriever
Golden Retriever
Great Dane
Labrador Retriever
Newfoundland
Rottweiler
St Bernard

HERDING DOGS
Australian Shepherd
Border Collie
Rough Collie
Old English Sheepdog
Shetland Sheepdog
Pembroke Welsh Corgi
Cardigan Welsh Corgi

SIGHT HOUNDS
Borzoi
Greyhound
Irish Wolfhound
Italian Greyhound
Scottish Deerhound
Whippet

SMALL TERRIERS
Australian Terrier
Boston Terrier
Briard
Cairn Terrier
Jack Russell
Norwich Terrier
Scottish Terrier
West Highland White Terrier
Yorkshire Terrier

today have arisen through hybridization between distinct dog breeds on separate occasions.

A group of Japanese researchers led by Akiko Tonoike was curious to find out whether spitzes and other older breeds displayed different behaviours from the modern breeds. They also wanted to investigate to what degree the behaviours varied between the different groups of modern dog breeds. Many of these dogs have been created through carefully controlled breeding over the past 150 years, so the researchers wondered whether the differences in behaviour have developed that much during this relatively short timespan.

In their study, published in the journal *Scientific Reports* in 2015, Tonoike and his colleagues started with the most recent group division of dogs based on genetic studies. They used a standardized survey called the C-BARQ, which had already been shown to be useful for evaluating behavioural problems in dogs. Dog owners in Japan and the USA answered 100 questions online about how their dogs had recently reacted to different events and stimuli.The researchers received a total of 2,951 answers from dog owners in Japan and 10,380 from owners in the USA. Analysis of this large amount of material showed a striking difference in behaviour between ancient and modern dogs in one respect: spitzes and the earlier breeds (Akita, Basenji, Samoyed, Siberian Husky and Shiba Inu) were less affectionate and didn't crave as much attention as contemporary breeds.

Their more reserved stance is probably a more primitive, wolf-like behaviour that has been chipped away through the breeding of contemporary dog breeds. Among the modern breeds, the group that included the Dobermann and German Shepherd deviated clearly from the other breeds. They were less afraid of unknown dogs, people and situations as well as less aggressive towards family members and not as anxious as other modern breed groups.

Because only pet dogs and no service dogs were in this study, these behaviours are probably inherited rather than learned. With regard to aggressiveness, a few dog groups stood out from the rest: dwarf dogs such as the Chihuahua, Pug, Papillon and Pomeranian showed more aggression towards unknown people and dogs, while the Labrador Retriever and Golden Retriever were among the least aggressive.

Because different domestic dogs have been bred for a clear purpose, we might expect to see obvious differences in behaviour between those bred for working and those that are just pets. But today, most dog breeds are used only as pets, regardless of what function they had in the past. Can we then still expect differences in dogs' behaviours in everyday life, and if so, in what way? These questions were recently investigated by a team of researchers led by Helena Eken Asp from Sweden's University of Agricultural Sciences. Just like the Japanese, the Swedish researchers used the C-BARQ survey and gathered information online about the behaviour of different breeds.

In total, 3,591 dogs were studied. They were divided into 11 breeds registered as working dogs with the Swedish Working Dog Association (Australian Shepherd, Australian Kelpie, Boxer, Briard, Dobermann, Hovawart, Malinois, Giant Schnauzer, Rottweiler, Tervueren and German Shepherd) and nine pet dog breeds (American Staffordshire Terrier, Bernese Mountain Dog, Chihuahua, Golden Retriever, Jack Russell Terrier, Lagotto Romagnolo, Nova Scotia Duck Tolling Retriever, Rhodesian Ridgeback and Shetland Sheepdog).

The differences in behaviour were clear: all the working dogs' typical behaviour was generally similar and clearly differed from the behaviour of pet dogs. Working dogs were more interested in playing with people, more easily trained and less anxious than pet dogs. It was also evident that there are differences in behaviour between the various dog breeds as well as between working dogs and pet dogs.

But are there any general behaviour patterns that differ between, for example, short-nosed and long-nosed dogs, tall and short or slim and stout dogs? In breeding for appearance, we may have also – consciously or unconsciously – contributed to certain behaviours becoming more distinct, at least if there is a genetic connection between appearance and behaviour. This is what the researcher Holly R. Stone with colleagues from Australia wanted to investigate with the help of a very large sample of material gathered from the Swedish Working Dog Association.

In this study, conducted between 1997 and 2014, there were 67,000 dogs in total from 45 different breeds. For the study, each dog walked with its owner and the test leader along a forest track. Along the path they encountered ten different scenarios in a predetermined order: contact, play, hunt, passive, play at a distance, sudden movement, metallic sound, ghost, play and pistol shots. A third person walked just behind the others and recorded the dog's reactions from a list of 33 different responses, measuring the intensity of each response on a five-point scale.

Clear patterns of behaviour emerged in this assessment: large dogs were more affectionate, cooperative and playful than small dogs, which showed more aggressive behaviour. Heavier dogs were braver, more curious and attentive than lighter dogs, which were more careful and nervous. In other words, the lighter and smaller the dog, the bigger was the risk for unwanted behaviours. Dog owners themselves have confirmed this result in other studies.

Researchers have also found, somewhat surprisingly, that short-nosed dogs are more interested in chasing small objects than long-nosed dogs. One would usually expect long-nosed breeds to be more interested in hunting. Several long-nosed dogs are incredibly fast after all, and willing to chase after prey; just think about the greyhound, for example, on the dog track! Previous research has also shown that short-nosed dogs in general interact more with their owner than long-nosed dogs, so maybe it's playfulness with the owner rather than the hunting instinct itself that is being measured in this test.

So far, researchers can only speculate about the possible reasons why behaviour differs between dogs with different body shapes. In some cases, it's because humans have consciously favoured certain behaviours in certain breeds. In other cases it could be that we've got certain behaviours into the bargain while the breeding has been focusing on a certain type of appearance. When there is a connection between appearance and behaviour, we could have subconsciously made certain dog breeds more playful or nervous, aggressive or sociable.

All dogs bred as working dogs must go through a behavioural assessment that analyses its different characteristics. How this test is conducted was described earlier in this chapter, but for this description of the dog's behaviour to be deemed an efficient tool for breeding work, the evaluated behaviours must be hereditary. But despite 40 years of research on this topic, there are still no conclusive answers to the question regarding whether the evaluated behaviours are hereditary. Some studies strongly suggest that certain behaviours are hereditary, while others have concluded that they are hereditary only for certain dog breeds.

To try to bring some clarity to the matter, a Czech research team conducted a meta-analysis, where the results from 48 published studies were analysed together. Lenka Hradecká and her colleagues discovered in this analysis that the tests made to measure dogs' behaviour don't work. But we do know that there are large differences in behaviours between dog breeds and various groups of dogs. Why doesn't this show when we're testing for the heritability of different behaviours? One possible explanation could be that it's not just inheritance that determines an adult dog's behaviour. The environment in which the puppy grows up is also a decisive factor in determining the stability of a behaviour pattern in the adult dog (see Chapter 1).

External environmental factors during the test event also have an impact on the result; these include the time of year when it was conducted, where the person who assessed the behaviour was standing in relation to the dog, what the weather was like during the test and so on. Lastly, it also matters if the dog has already practised the elements that make up the behavioural assessment. For all these reasons, there is a risk that behavioural assessments are a blunt instrument when determining whether or not a dog is suitable for breeding.

Knowing how different dog breeds are related is not just of academic interest, but can also help researchers find cures for diseases that afflict both dogs and humans. So wrote Heidi G. Parker and Samuel F. Gilbert in an article published in *Advances in Genomics and Genetics* in 2016.

Researchers often use mice to study various genetic diseases. But the dog is a better model for two reasons: firstly because the human is more closely related to the dog than the mouse, and secondly because we have as many as 360 different diseases in common with the dog – diabetes, epilepsy and cancer among others. It's both quicker and cheaper to find the causes of inherited diseases with the dog than the human.

Since certain genetic diseases afflict only certain dog breeds – for example the bone cancer osteosarcoma in the Rottweiler – the genetic variation is more limited, which means that researchers can focus more easily on the search. There are examples where genetic mapping of a disease in dogs – for example narcolepsy in the Dobermann and Labrador Retriever – later led to the discovery of mutations on the corresponding genes in humans.

More recently, muscular dystrophy (when the muscles gradually weaken and waste away) has been successfully treated in Golden Retrievers with the help of gene therapy, which is good news for future treatment of this disease in humans. The dog is truly man's best friend in many ways!

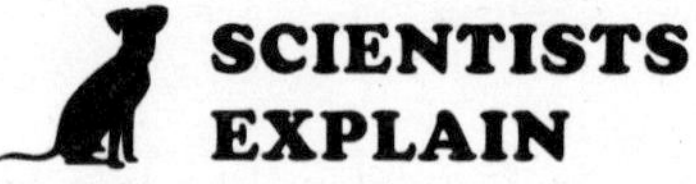

Dog breeds

- Today there are more than 400 dog breeds, each with their own breed standard. The largest breeds are about 50 times heaver and ten times taller than the smallest breeds.
- Modern genetic research shows that spitzes and other ancient breeds are the original dogs. They are generally not as affectionate or attention-seeking as modern breeds.
- Domestic working dog breeds are generally more interested in playing with humans, willing to be trained and less afraid than pet dogs bred as companions.

- Large dogs are usually more affectionate, cooperative and playful than small dogs. Heavier dogs are braver, more curious and attentive than lighter dogs.
- Lighter and smaller dogs pose the greatest risk for unwanted behaviours.
- Short-nosed dogs interact more with their owner than long-nosed dogs.
- Assessing the behaviour of a dog to determine its breed characteristics is a blunt instrument in deciding whether or not the dog is suitable for breeding.
- The human has 360 different diseases in common with the dog. Mapping and treatment of inherited diseases in dogs can therefore also help us humans.

Free-roaming dogs

If someone called your mongrel dog a mutt, you might take offence. While the word 'mutt' is often used in a derogatory way today, the word first appeared in the nineteenth century and simply meant a dog of indeterminate breed that ran loose rather than being confined and controlled by humans, and often distinguishing itself by being aggressive and barking. These free-roaming or free-ranging dogs, often known as village or street dogs, are not domesticated but neither are they wild like feral dogs.

There are hardly any village dogs in the more developed countries, but if we look elsewhere they're still common. In fact, 80 per cent of the world's 900 million dogs could be categorized as village dogs, and most of them are obviously in the warmer parts of the world, such as South America, Africa and South Asia. These dogs roam freely in towns and villages where they feed predominantly off our rubbish, even if they might be loosely tied to one or several households. Street dogs in cities, on the other hand, are completely stray.

The life of a village or street dog is radically different from that of a pet dog. Village dogs and street dogs live a miserable and dangerous life: over 60 per cent of their puppies die, and those that do survive to adulthood live on average for only three or four years. In India, leopards come into villages and towns under cover of darkness and dogs are their main prey. In Maharashtra in West India, for example, the researcher Vidya Athreya and her colleagues analysed hair from samples of leopard faeces and found that dog hair was prevalent in almost 40 per cent of all the samples, despite the density of goats in the area being seven times higher than dogs'. While the village dogs are roaming freely day and night, the goats are more protected by people – shepherds watch them during the day and they live in guarded shelters at night.

But if dogs are the leopard's prey, what do village dogs live on? Clues to the answer came from another Indian study, led by Abhishek Ghoshal, in Himachal Pradesh on the Himalayan border. In the past two decades the area has become increasingly popular for walking tourism in the mountains, and the number of restaurants and hotels has therefore increased tenfold in Himachal Pradesh during that time. More people mean more waste, which leads to more village dogs since there's plenty of food available for them to scavenge. Their increasing numbers have now become a threat both to livestock and to wild animals in the neighbouring nature reserves.

The same goes for southern Chile, where it's believed that village dogs stray into protected areas in their hunt for food. But how big is the problem? Maybe the dogs keep close to the villages after all? To answer these questions, researcher Maximiliano Sepúlveda attached GPS collars to 14 dogs. The collars showed that these dogs searched for food outside the village for only an hour a day; most didn't venture farther than 500 to 1,900 metres from the village and they kept to roads, rivers and open fields, avoiding forests unless there were wide pathways. During the remaining 23 hours they stayed within 200 metres of the village.

These results show that these particular village dogs didn't pose any great danger to wild animals in the surrounding nature areas. The researchers noticed, however, that dogs occasionally moved unhindered across larger distances, despite having an owner waiting for them at home.

In the USA and Europe, are dogs that run loose considered a threat to wildlife? In many states in the USA dogs must always be on a lead outdoors, whereas in the UK, for example, it isn't always necessary (but they must be kept on a lead in pedestrian areas and on land where livestock is present). Most people are aware that dogs should be under close control at all times when we walk in nature, even if there is no absolute constraint on using a lead.

But in some countries hunting with hounds is an exception in the law. In Sweden, for example, two studies have investigated how deer and elk behave when they have hounds chasing them. Anders Jarnemo and Camilla Wikenros at the Grimsö research station studied how deer behaved in the deep forests of Kolmården during three hunting seasons. Nine roe hinds and four bucks had been provided with a GPS collar and the researchers could therefore follow their movements in detail when the hunting dogs – either pure German Spaniels or a mix between German Spaniels and Norwegian Elkhound – came into their vicinity.

The GPS collars showed that the bucks ran off 5 kilometres when the hunting dogs approached, while the hinds ran half as far. The animal that ran the farthest was a hind that ran 15 kilometres away. In general, it took them almost a day to return to their home area. In a similar study in Denmark, it took the deer up to five days to return, which might be because the landscape there is more open than Kolmården's forests and deer are usually wary of moving out into open fields. When the hunt in Kolmården was repeated the following week, the deer ran away faster than they did in the previous week. They were obviously more watchful this time around.

But perhaps the king of the forest, the elk, isn't as intimidated by a small dog barking? Elk in North America even confront attacking wolves, and if the wolves are few or the depth of snow makes attack difficult, the wolves would rather retreat than risk injuring themselves. Do elk react in the same way to dogs as

they do to wolves? Do they stay and fight the barking dogs, as in North America, or do they run away?

To answer these questions, Göran Ericsson and colleagues from the University of Agricultural Sciences in Umeå studied how ten elk cows with GPS collars reacted to hounds hunting outside Lycksele in northern Sweden. In 80 per cent of cases the elk fled when the Norwegian Elkhounds approached. They ran on average more than 3 kilometres as the crow flies, but the actual distance was double that because they zigzagged in an orderly fashion across the terrain. If, however, the elk became aware of the dog when it was 100 metres away, it would run straight ahead without any manoeuvres. Just like the deer, the elk became extra watchful after the first incident.

Researchers concluded that the elk have learned that there's no point challenging a barking dog because the chance of avoiding the hunters' bullets is very small. In that way, elk have adapted to a life where humans and their dogs, and not the wolf, are the biggest threat in the Swedish forests.

Maybe the elk's behaviour will adapt in the future if the number of wolves is allowed to grow. The number of wolves in Sweden today is one per thousand of the elk population, while there are almost as many hunters as there are elk.

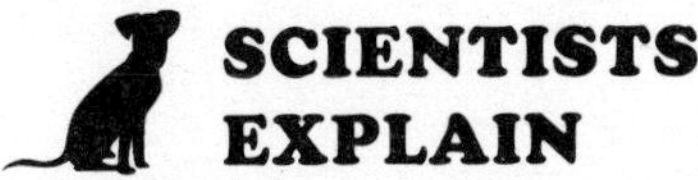

Free-roaming dogs

- There are an estimated 900 million dogs in the world, about 80 per cent of which are village (or street) dogs. These are dogs that run loose in towns and villages and predominantly live off rubbish even if they're loosely tied to one or several households.
- More than 60 per cent of village dog puppies die and their average life expectancy is just three to four years.
- Increased tourism creates more refuse, which leads to more village dogs. In some parts of the world these dogs may be a threat to both livestock and wild animals. However, most village dogs don't venture far from the villages.
- When hunting with a roaming dog, deer can escape up to 5 kilometres and it usually takes them a day to return to their home area. The elk runs away from a barking dog as well, usually about 3 kilometres away as the crow flies.

References

Introduction

Brodrej, G. 2015. 'Hunden är kvinnans klimakteriesladdis' [The dog is the woman's menopause]. *Expressen* 17 June. www.expressen.se/kultur/hunden-ar-klimakteriekvinnans-sladdbarn/

European Pet Food Industry Federation (FEDIAF) 2012. Facts & Figures 2012.

Hellberg, A. 2013. 'Hunden, det nya barnet' [The dog, the new child]. *Unt* 8 April. http://www.unt.se/leva/hunden-det-nya-barnet-2363061.aspx

Statistiska Centralbyrån [Central Bureau of Statistics] 2012. 'Hundar, katter och andra sällskapsdjur [Dogs, cats and other pets] 2012.'

1 The sociable dog

Your puppy's social development

Foyer, P. et al. 2016. 'Levels of maternal care in dogs affect adult offspring temperament.' – *Scientific Reports* 6:19253. doi: 10.1038/srep19253

Howell, T. J. et al. 2015. 'Puppy parties and beyond: The role of early age socialization practices on adult dog behavior.' – *Veterinary Medicine: Research and Reports* 6: 143–153. doi: 10.2147/VMRR.s62081

Morrow, M. et al. 2015. 'Breed-dependent differencesin the onset of fear-related avoidance behavior in puppies.' – *Journal of Veterinary Behavior* 10: 286–294. doi: 10.1016/j.jveb.2015.03.002

Robinson, L. M. et al. 2016. 'Puppy temperament assessments predict breed and American Kennel Club group but not adult temperament.' – *Journal of Applied Animal Welfare Science.* doi: 10.1080/10888705.2015.1127765

Personality tests

McGarrity, M. E. et al. 2015. 'Which personality dimensions do puppy test measure? A systematic procedure for categorizing behavioral assays.' – *Behavioural Processes* 110: 117–124. doi: 10.1016/j.beproc.2014.09.029

Nagasawa, M. et al. 2016. 'Comparison of behavioral characteristics of dogs in the United States and Japan.' – *Journal of Veterinary Medical Science* 78: 231–238. doi: 10.1292/jvms.15-0253

Roth, L. S. V. & Jensen, P. 2015. 'Assessing companion dog behavior in a social setting.' – *Journal of Veterinary Behavior* 10: 315–323. doi:10.1016/j. jveb.2015.04.003

Dog play

Bradshaw, J. W. S. et al. 2015. 'Why do adult dogs "play"?' *Behavioural Processes* 110: 82–87. doi: 10.1016/j.beproc.2014.09.023

Byosiere S.-E. et al. 2016. 'Investigating the function of play bows in adult pet dogs (*Canis lupus familiaris*).' – *Behavioural Processes* 125: 106–113. doi: 10.1016/j.beproc.2016.02.007

Norman, K. M. 2011. 'Down but not out: Supine postures as facilitators of play in domestic dogs.' PhD thesis, University of Lethbridge, Canada.

Hierarchy and dominance

Bradshaw, J. W. S. et al. 2009. 'Dominance in dogs: Useful construct or bad habit?' *Journal of Veterinary Behavior* 3: 176–177. doi: 10.1016/j.jveb.2008.08.004

Pal, S. K. 2014. 'Factors influencing intergroup atagonistic behaviour in free-ranging domestic dogs (*Canis familiaris*).' – *Acta Ethologica.* doi: 10.1007/s10211-014-0208-2

Trisko, R. K. & Smuts, B. B. 2015. 'Dominance relationships in a group of domestic dogs (*Canis lupus familiaris*).' – *Behaviour* 152: 677–704. doi: 10.1163/1568539X-00003249

van der Borg, J. A. M. et al. 2015. 'Dominance in domestic dogs: A quantitative analysis of its behavioural measures.' – *PLoS ONE* 10: e0133978. doi:10.1371/journal.pone.0133978

2 The dog–human relationship

Bonding

Brown, C. M. & McLean, J. L. 2015. 'Anthropomorphizing dogs: Projecting one's own personality and consequences for supporting animal rights.' – *Anthrozoos* 28: 73–86. doi: 10.2752/089279315 X14129350721975

Feurbacher, E. N. & Wynne, C. D. L. 2015. 'Shut up and pet me! Domestic dogs (*Canis lupus familiaris*) prefer petting to vocal praise in concurrent and single-alternative choice procedures.' – *Behavioural Processes* 110: 47–59. doi: 10.1016/j.beproc.2014.08.019

Gray, P. B. et al. 2015. 'The roles of pet dogs and cats in human courtship and dating.' – *Anthrozoos* 28: 673–683. doi: 10.1080/08927936.2015.1064216

Payne, E. et al. 2015. 'Exploring the existence and potential underpinnings of dog–human and horse–human attachment bonds.' – *Behavioural Processes.* doi: 10.1016/j.beproc.2015.10.004

Payne, E. et al. 2015. 'Current perspectives on attachment and bonding in the dog–human dyad.' – *Psychology Research and Behavior Management* 8: 71–79. doi: 10.2147/PRBM.S74972

Thorn, P. et al. 2015. 'The canine cuteness effect: Owner-perceived cuteness as a predictor of human-dog relationship quality.' – *Anthrozoos* 28: 569–585. doi: 10.1080/08927936.2015.1069992

How does your dog feel about you?

Albuquerque, N. et al. 2016. 'Dogs recognize dog and human emotions.' – *Biology Letters* 12:20150883. doi: 10.1098/rsbl.2015.0883

Carballo, F. et al. 2015. 'Dogs's discrimination of human selfish and generous attitudes: The role of individual recognition, experience, and experimenters' gender.' – *PLoS ONE* 10: e0116314. doi: 10.1371/journal.pone.0116314

Cuaya, L. V. et al. 2016. 'Our faces in the dog's brain: Functional imaging reveals temporal cortex activation during perception of human faces.' – *PLoS ONE* 11: e-0149431. doi: 10.1371/journal.pone.0149431

Kerepsi, A. et al. 2014. 'Dogs and their human companions: The effect of familiarity on dog–human interactions.' – *Behavioural Processes.* doi: 10.1016/j.beproc.2014.02.005

Yong, M. H. & Ruffman, T. 2015. 'Domestic dogs match human male voices to faces, but not for females.' – *Behaviour*. doi: 10.1163/1568539X-00003294

Assistance and service dogs

Fadel, F. R. et al. 2016. 'Differences in trait impulsivity indicate diversification of dog breeds into working and show lines.' – *Scientific Reports* 6:22162. doi: 10.1037/srep22162

Fishman, G. A. 2003. 'When your eyes have a wet nose: The evolution of the use of guide dogs and establishing the seeing eye.' – *Survey of Ophthalmology* 48: 452–458. doi: 10.1016/s0039-6257(03)00052-3

Foyer, P. et al. 2016. 'Behavior and cortisol responses of dogs evaluated in a standardized temperament test for military working dogs.' – *Journal of Veterinary Behavior* 11: 7–12. doi: 10.1016/j. jveb.2015.09.006

Hall, S. S. et al. 2016. 'What factors are associated with positive effects of dog ownership in families with children with autism spectrum disorder? The development of the Lincoln Autism Pet Dog Impact Scale.' – *PLoS ONE* 11: e0149736. doi: 10.1371/journal.pone.0149736

Harvey, N. D. et al. 2016. 'Test-retest reliability and predictive validity of a juvenile guide dog behavior test.' – *Journal of Veterinary Behavior* 11: 65–76. doi: 10-1016/j.jveb.2015.09.005

Jackson, M. M. et al. 2015. 'Fido – Facilitating interactions for dogs with occupations: Wearable communication interfaces for working dogs.' – *Personal and Ubiquitous Computing* 19: 155–173. doi: 10.1007/s00779-014-0817-9

Mongillo, P. et al. 2015. 'Validation of a selection protocol of dogs involved in animal-assisted intervention.' – *Journal of Veterinary Behavior* 10: 103–110. doi: 10.1016/j.jveb.2014.11.005

Government official investigations 2010. 'A better market for service dogs.' Report by the Service Dog Breeders' Investigation. SOU 2010:21.

Stevenson, K. et al. 2015. 'Can a dog be used as a motivator to develop social interaction and engagement with teachers for students with autism?' *Nasen.* doi: 10.1111/1467-9604-12105

Swall, A. et al. 2014. 'Can therapy dogs evoke awareness of one's past and present life in persons with Alzheimer's disease?' *International Journal of Older People Nursing.* doi: 10.1111/opn.12053

Yamamoto, M. et al. 2015. 'Registrations of assistance dogs in California for identification tags: 1999–2012.' – *PLoS ONE* 10: e0132820. doi: 10.1371/journal.pone.0132820

Healthy dog walks

Engelberg, J. K. et al. 2016. 'Dog walking among adolescents: Correlates and contribution to physical activity.' – *Preventive Medicine* 82: 65–72. doi: 10.1016/j.ypmed.2015.11.011

Garcia, D. O. et al. 2015. 'Relationships between dog ownership and physical activity in postmenopausal women.' – *Preventive Medicine.* doi: 10.1016.j.ypmed.2014.10.030

Richards, E. A. 2015. 'Prevalence of dog walking and sociodemographic characteristics of dog walkers in the U.S.: An update from 2001.' – *American Journal of Health Behavior.* 39: 500–506. doi: 10.5993./AJHB.39.4.6

Schneider, K. L. et al. 2014. 'An online social network to increase walking in dog owners: A randomized trial.' – *Medicine & Science in Sports and Exercise.* doi: 10.1249/mss.0000000000000441

Westgarth, C. et al. 2015. 'Factors associated with daily walking of dogs.' – *BMC Veterinary Research* 11: 116. doi: 10.1186/s12917-015-0434-5

3 Communicating with your dog

The attentive dog

Bálint, A. et al. 2015. '"Do not choose as I do!" – Dogs avoid the food that is indicated by another dog's gaze in a two-object choice task.' – *Applied Animal Behaviour Science* 170: 44–53. doi: 10.1016/j.applanim.2015.06.005

Buttner, A. P. et al. 2015. 'Evidence for a synchronization of hormonal states between humans and dogs during competition.' – *Physiology & Behavior* 147: 54–62. doi: 10.1016/j.physbeh.2015.04.010

Chijiiwa, H. et al. 2015. 'Dogs avoid people who behave negatively to their owner: Third-party affective evaluation.' – *Animal Behaviour* 106: 123–127. doi: 10.1016/j.anbehav.2015.05.018

Duranton, C. et al. 2016. 'When facing an unfamiliar person, pet dogs present social referencing based on their owners' direction of movement alone.' – *Animal Behaviour* 113: 147–156. doi: 10.1016/j.anbehav.2016.01.004

Fugazza, C. & Miklósi, Á. 2015. 'Social learning in dog training: The effectiveness of the Do as I do method compared to shaping/clicker training.' – *Applied Animal Behaviour Science*. doi: 10.1016/j.applanim.2015.08.033

Gerencsér, L. et al. 2016. 'The effect of reward-handler dissociation on dog's obedience performance in different conditions.' – *Applied Animal Behaviour Science* 174: 103–110. doi: 10.1016/j.applanim.2015.11.009

Konok, V. et al. 2014. 'How do humans represent emotion of dogs? The resemblance between the human representation of the canine and the human affective space.' – *Applied Animal Behaviour Science.* doi: 10.1016/j.applanim.2014.11.003

Ostojíc, L. et al. 2015. 'Are owners' reports of their dogs' "guilty look" influenced by the dogs' action and evidence of the misdeed?' *Behavioural Processes* 111: 97–100. doi: 10.1016/j.behproc.2014.12.010

Persson, M. E. et al. 2015. 'Human-directed social behaviour in dogs shows significant heritability.' – *Genes, Brain and Behavior.* doi: 10.1111/gbb.12194

Turcsán, B. et al. 2014. 'Fetching what the owner prefers? Dogs recognize disgust and happiness in human behaviour.' – *Animal Cognition.* doi: 10.1007/s10071-014-0779-3

Yong, M. H. & Ruffman, T. 2014. 'Is that fear? Domestic dogs' use of social referencing signals from an unfamiliar person.' – *Behavioural Processes.* doi: 10.1016/j.beproc.2014.09.018

Finger pointing

Flom, R. & Gartman, P. 2015. 'Does affective information influence domestic dogs' (*Canis lupus familiaris*) point-following behavior?' *Animal Cognition.* doi: 1007/s10071-015-0934-5

Lazarowski, L. & Dorman, D. C. 2015. 'A comparison of pet and purpose-bred research dogs (*Canis familiaris*) performance on human-guided object-choice tasks.' – *Behavioural Processes* 110: 60–67. doi: 10.1016/j.beproc.2014.09.021

Moore, R. et al. 2015. 'Two-year-old children but not domestic dogs understand communicative intentions without language, gestures, or gaze.' – *Developmental Science* 18: 232–242. doi: 10.1111/desc.12206

Takaoka, A. et al. 2015. 'Do dogs follow behavioral cues from an unreliable human?' *Animal Cognition* 18: 475–483. doi: 10.1007/s10071-014-0816-2

Tauzin, T. et al. 2015. 'What or where? The meaning of referential human pointing for dogs (*Canis familiaris*).' – *Journal of Comparative Psychology*. doi: 10.1037/a0039462

Yoon, J. M. D. et al. 2008. 'Communication-induced memory biases in preverbal infants.' – *Proceedings of the National Academy of Sciences*, USA 105:13690–13695. doi: 10.1073/pnas.0804388105

Eye contact

d'Aniello, B. & Scandurra, A. 2016. 'Ontogenetic effects on gazing behaviour: A case study of kennel dogs (Labrador Retrievers) in the impossible task paradigm.' – *Animal Cognition*. doi: 10.1007/s10071-016-0958-5

d'Aniello, B. et al. 2014. 'Gazing towards humans: A study on water rescue dogs using the impossible task paradigm.' – *Behavioural Processes*. doi: 10.1016/j.beproc.2014.09.022

Gaunet, F. 2008. 'How do guide dogs of blind owners and pet dogs of sighted owners (*Canis familiaris*) ask their owners for food?' *Animal Cognition* 11: 475–483

Hernádi, A. et al. 2015. 'Intranasally administered oxytoin affects how dogs (*Canis familiaris*) react to the threatening approach of their owner and an unfamiliar experimenter.' – *Behavioural Processes* 119: 1–5. doi: 10.1016/j.beproc. 2015-07.001

Nagasawa, M. et al. 2015. 'Oxytocin-gaze positive loop and the coevolution of human–dog bonds.' – *Science* 348: 333–336. doi: 10.1126/science. 1261022

Ohkita, M. et al. 2016. 'Owners' direct gazes increase dogs' attention-getting behaviors.' – *Behavioural Processes*. doi: 10.1016/j.beproc.2016.02.013

Oliva, J. L. et al. 2015. 'Oxytocin enhances the appropriate use of human social cues by the domestic dog (*Canis familiaris*) in an object choice task.' – *Animal Cognition*. doi: 10.1007/s10071-015-0843-7

Persson, M. E. et al. 2015. 'Human-directed social behaviour in dogs shows significant heritability.' – *Genes, Brain and Behavior*. doi: 10.1111/gbb.12194

Romero, T. et al. 2015. 'Intranasal administration of oxytocin promotes social play in domestic dogs.' – *Communicative & Integrative Biology* 8: e1017157. doi: 10.1080/19420889.2015.1017157

Scandurra, A. et al. 2015. 'Guide dogs as a model for investigating the effect of life experience and training on gazing behaviour.' – *Animal Cognition* 18: 937–944. doi: 10.1007/s10071-015-0864-2

Törnqvist, H. et al. 2016. 'Comparison of dogs and humans in visual scanning of social interaction.' – *Royal Society Open Science* 2: 150341. doi: 10.1098/rsos.150341

Wallis, L. J. et al. 2015. 'Training for eye contact modulates gaze following in dogs.' – *Animal Behaviour* 106: 27–35. doi: 10.1016/j.anbehav.2015.04.020

4 Problem solving

Behavioural problems

Chung, T.-h. et al. 2015. 'Prevalence of canine behavior problems related to dog–human relationship in South Korea: A pilot study.' – *Journal of Veterinary Behavior*. doi: 10.1016/j.jveb.2015.10.003

Pirrone, F. et al. 2016. 'Owner-reported aggressive behavior towards familiar people may be a more prominent occurrence in pet shop-traded dogs.' – *Journal of Veterinary Behavior* 11: 13–17. doi: 10.1016/j.jveb.2015.11.007

Vanderstichel, R. et al. 2014. 'Changes in blood testosterone concentrations following surgical and chemical sterilization of male free-roaming dogs in southern Chile.' – *Theriogenology*. doi: 10.1016/j.theriogenology.2014.12.001

Fear, worry and anxiety

Karagiannis, C. I. et al. 2015. 'Dogs with separation-related problems show a "less pessimistic" cognitive bias during treatment with fluoxetine (Reconcile™) and a behaviour modification plan.' – *BMC Veterinary Research* 11: 80. doi: 10.1186/s12917-015-0373-1

Koda, N. et al. 2015. 'Stress levels in dogs, and its recognition by their handlers, during animal-assisted therapy in a prison.' – *Animal Welfare* 24: 203–209. doi: 10.7120/09627286.24.2.203

Nicholson, S. L. & Meredith, J. E. 2015. 'Should stress management be part of the clinical care provided to chronically ill dogs?' *Journal of Veterinary Behavior*. doi: 10.1016/j.jveb.2015.09.002

Notari, L. et al. 2015. 'Behavioural changes in dogs treated with corticosteroids.' – *Physiology & Behaviour* 151: 609–616. doi: 10.1016/j.physbeh. 2015.08.041

Sandri, M. et al. 2015. 'Salivary cortisol concentration in healthy dogs is affected by size, sex, and housing context.' – *Journal of Veterinary Behavior* 10: 302–306. doi: 10.1016.j.jveb.2015.03.011

Tiira, K. & Lohi, H. 2015. 'Early life experiences and exercise associate with canine anxieties.' – *PLoS ONE* 10: e0141907. doi: 10.1371/journal. pone.0141907

Travain, T. et al. 2015. 'Hot dogs: Thermography in the assessment of stress in dogs (*Canis familiaris*) – A pilot study.' – *Journal of Veterinary Behavior* 10: 17–23. doi: 10.1016/j.jveb.2014.11.003

My dog isn't dangerous ...

Lakestani, N. & Donaldson, M. L. 2015. 'Dog bite prevention: Effect of a short educational intervention for preschool children.' – *PLoS ONE* 10: e0134319. doi: 10.1371/journal.pone.0134319

Matos, R. E. et al. 2015. 'Characteristics and risk factors of dog aggression in the Slovak Republic.' – *Veterinarni Medicina* 60: 432–445. doi: 10.17221/8418-vetmed

Matthias, J. et al. 2014. 'Cause, setting and ownership analysis of dog bites in Bay County, Florida from 2009 to 2010.' – *Zoonoses and Public Health.* doi: 10.1111/zph.12115

McMillan, F. D. et al. 2015. 'Behavioral and psychological characteristics of canine victims of abuse.' – *Journal of Applied Animal Welfare Science* 18: 92–111. doi:10.1080/10888705.2014.962230

Mongillo, P. et al. 2015. 'Attention of dogs and owners in urban contexts: Public perception and problematic behaviors.' – *Journal of Veterinary Behavior*, doi: 10.1016/j.jveb.2015.01.004

Orritt, R. et al. 2015. 'His bark is worse than his bite: Perceptions and rationalization of canine aggressive behavior.' – *Human–Animal Interaction Bulleting* 3: 1–20.

Overall, K. L. 2001. 'Dog bites to humans: Demography, epidemiology, injury, and risk.' – *Journal of the American Veterinary Medical Association* 218: 1924–1934.

Pirrone, F. et al. 2015. 'Owner and animal factors predict the incidence of, and owner reaction towards, problem behaviors in companion dogs.' – *Journal of Veterinary Behavior*. doi: 10.1016/j.jveb.2015.03.004

Rezac, P. et al. 2015. 'Human behavior preceding dog bites to the face.' – *The Veterinary Journal*. doi: 10.1016/j.tvjl.2015.10.021

Räddningsverket (Rescue Work). 2008. 'Därför biter hundar människor' [So dogs bite people]. nco 2008-05-05.

Seligsohn, D. 2014. 'Dog bite incidence and associated risk factors: A cross-sectional study on schoolchildren in Tamil Nadu.' Master's thesis 2014:20. issn 1652-8697. Swedish University of Agricultural Sciences.

The Swedish Civil Contingencies Agency. 2015. 'Dogs and accidents.' Facts 2015-07-08. MSB-89.5

Westgarth, C. & Watkins, F. 2015. 'A qualitative investigation of the perceptions of female dog-bite victims and implications for the prevention of dog bites.' – *Journal of Veterinary Behavior* 10: 479–488. doi: 10.1016/j. jveb.2015.07.035

Homeless dogs

Dudley, E. S. et al. 2015. 'Effects of repeated petting sessions on leukocyte counts, intestinal parasite prevalence, and plasma cortisol concentration of dogs housed in a county animal shelter.' – *Journal of the American Veterinary Medical Association* 247: 1289–1298.

Kiddie, J. & Collins, L. 2015. 'Identifying environmental and management factors that may be associated with the quality of life of kenneled dogs (*Canis familiaris*).' – *Applied Animal Behaviour Science* 167: 43–55. doi: 10.1016/j.applanim. 2015. 03.007

Lambert, K. et al. 2014. 'A systematic review and meta-analysis of the proportion of dogs surrendered for dog-related and owner-related reasons.' – *Preventive Veterinary Medicine.* doi: 10.1016/j. prevetmed.2014.11.002

Mornement, K. M. et al. 2015. 'Evaluation of the predictive validity of the Behavioural Assessment for Rehoming K9s (BARK) protocol and owner satisfaction with adopted dogs.' – *Applied Animal Behaviour Science* 167: 35–42. doi: 10.1016/j. applanim.2015.03.013

Protopopova, A. 2016. 'Effects of sheltering on physiology, immune function, behavior, and the welfare of dogs.' – *Physiology & Behavior* 159: 95–103. doi: 10.1016/j.physbeh. 2016.03.020

Protopopova, A. et al. 2016. 'Preference assessments and structured potential adopter-dog interactions increase adoptions.' – *Applied Animal Behaviour Science* 176: 87–95. doi: 10.1016/j. applanim. 2015.12.003

Rydberg, C. 2009. 'Utredning och uppföljning av adoptionshundars situation' [Investigation and follow-up of adopted dogs]. Student work 276. Department of Animal Environment and Health, Swedish Agricultural University.

Zák, J. et al. 2015. 'Sex, age and size as factors affecting the length of stay of dogs in Czech shelters.' – *Acta Veterinaria Brno* 84: 407–413. doi: 10.2754/avb201584040407

5 Your dog's health

Eternal youth?

Creevy, K. E. et al. 2016. 'The companion dog as a model for the longevity dividend.' – *Cold Spring Harbor Perspectives in Medicine* 6:a026633. doi: 10.1101/chsperspect.a026633

Evert, J. et al. 2003. 'Morbidity profiles of centenarians: Survivors, delayers, and escapers.' – *Journals of Gerontology* Series A 58: 232–237. doi: 10.1093/gerona/58.3.M232

Hoffman, J. M. et al. 2013. 'Reproductive capability is associated with lifespan and cause of death in companion dogs.' – *PLoS ONE* 8: e61082. doi: 10.1371/journal.pone.0061082

O'Neill, D. G. et al. 2013. 'Longevity and mortality of owned dogs in England.' – *The Veterinary Journal* 198: 638–643. doi: 10.1016/j.tvjl.2013.09.020

Youssef, S. A. et al. 2016. 'Pathology of the aging brain in domestic and laboratory animals, and animal models of human neurodegenerative diseases.' – *Veterinary Pathology* 53: 327–348. doi: 10.1177/0300985815623997

Excess weight and obesity

Ohtani, N. et al. 2015. 'Increased feeding speed is associated with higher subsequent sympathetic activity in dogs.' – *PLoS ONE* 10: e142899. doi: 10.1371/journal.pone.0142899

Raffan, E. et al. 2015. 'Development, factor structure and application of the Dog Obesity Risk and Appetite (dora) questionnaire.' – *PeerJ* 3: e1278. doi: 10.7717/peerj.1278

Raffan, E. et al. 2016. 'A deletion in the canine POMC gene is associated with weight and appetite in obesity-prone Labrador Retriever dogs.' – *Cell Metabolism* 23: 893–900. doi: 10.1016/j.cmet.2016.04.012

Bacteria, viruses and parasites

Curi, N. H. A. et al. 2016. 'Prevalence and risk factors for viral exposure in rural dogs around protected areas of the Atlantic forest.' – *BMC Veterinary Research* 12:21. doi: 10.1186/s12917-016-0646-3

Smith, A. F. et al. 2015. 'Urban park-related risks for *Giardia* spp. infection in dogs.' – *Epidemiological Infections* 143: 3277–3291. doi: 10.1017/s0950268815000400

Smith, A. F. et al. 2015. 'Reported off-leash frequency and perception of risk for gastrointestinal parasitism are not associated in owners of urban park-attending dogs: A multifactorial investigation.' – *Preventive Veterinary Medicine* 120: 336–348. doi: 10.1016/j.prevetmed.2015.03.017

Wera, E. et al. 2016. 'Intention of dog owners to participate in rabies control measures in Flores Island, Indonesia.' – *Preventive Veterinary Medicine*. doi: 10.1016/j.prevetmed.2016.02.029

6 Your dog's senses

The sense of smell

Hall, N. J. et al. 2015. 'Performance of Pugs, German Shepherds, and Greyhounds (*Canis lupus familiaris*) on an odor-discrimination task.' – *Journal of Comparative Psychology*. doi: 10.1037/a0039271

Hamilton, J. & Vonk, J. 2015. 'Do dogs (*Canis lupus familiaris*) prefer family?' – *Behavioural Processes*. doi: 10.1016/j.beproc.2015.08.004

Johansson, P. 2009. 'Hundens kommunikationssignaler' [The dog's communication signals]. Student work 276. Department of Animal Environment and Health, Swedish Agricultural University.

Polgár, Z. et al. 2015. 'Strategies used by pet dogs for solving olfaction-based problems at various distances.' – *PLoS ONE* 10: e0131610. doi: 10.1371/journal. pone.0131610

Music for all

Bowman, A. et al. 2015. '"Four Seasons" in an animal rescue centre; Classical music reduces environmental stress in kennelled dogs.' – *Physiology & Behavior.* doi: 10.1016/j.physbeh.2015.02.035

Brayley, C. & Montrose, T. 2015. 'The effects of audiobooks on the behaviour of dogs at a rehoming kennels.' – *Applied Animal Behaviour Science.* doi: 10.1016/j.applanim.2015.11.008

Right or left?

Gough, W. & McGuire, B. 2015. 'Urinary posture and motor laterality in dogs (Canis lupus familiaris) at two shelters.' – *Applied Animal Behaviour Science* 168: 61–70. doi: 10.1016.j.applanim.2015.04-006

Siniscalchi, M. et al. 2016. 'The dog nose "KNOWS" fear: Asymmetric nostril use during sniffing at canine and human emotional stimuli.' – *Behavioural Brain Research* 304: 34–41. doi: 10.1016/j. bbr.2016.02.011

Wells, D. L. et al. 2016. 'Comparing lateral bias in dogs and humans using the Kong™ ball test.' – *Applied Animal Behaviour Science* 176: 70–76. doi: 10.1016/j.applanim.2016.01.010

7 How dogs originated

The dog and the wolf

Axelsson E. et al. 2013. 'The genomic signature of dog domestication reveals adaptation to a starch-rich diet.' – *Nature* 495: 360–365. doi: 10.1038/nature11837

Bradshaw, J. W. S. et al. 2016. 'Dominance in domestic dogs: A response to Schilder et al. (2014).' – *Journal of Veterinary Behavior.* 11: 102–108. doi: 10.1016/j.jveb.2015.11.008

Cagan, A. & Blass, T. 2016. 'Identification of genomic variants putatively targeted by selection during dog domestication.' –

BMC Evolutionary Biology 16:10. doi: 10.1186/s12862-015-0579-7

Freedman, A. H. et al. 2014. 'Genome sequencing highlights the dynamic early history of dogs.' – *PLoS Genetics* 10: e1004016. doi: 10.1371/journal.pgen.1004016

Kopaliani, N. et al. 2014. 'Gene flow between wolf and shepherd dog populations in Georgia (Caucasus).' – *Journal of Heredity*. doi: 10.1093/jhered/esu014

Li, Y. et al. 2014. 'Domestication of the dog from the wolf was promoted by enhanced excitatory synaptic plasticity: A hypothesis.' – *Genome Biology and Evolution* 6: 3115–3121. doi: 10.1093/gbe/evu245

Marshall-Pescini, S. et al. 2015. 'The effect of domestication on inhibitory control: Wolves and dogs compared.' – *PLoS ONE*. doi: 10.1371/journal.pone.0118469

Mehrkam, L. R. & Thompson, R. K. R. 2015. 'Seasonal trends in intrapack aggression of captive wolves (*Canis lupus*) and wolf-dog crosses: Implications for management of mixed-subspecies exhibits.' – *Journal of Applied Animal Welfare Science* 18: 1–16. doi: 10.1080.10888705.2014.923773

Moretti, L. et al. 2015. 'The influence of relationships on neophobia and exploration in wolves and dogs.' – *Animal Behaviour* 107: 159–173. doi: 10.1016. j.anbehav.2015.06.008

Parker, H. G. & Gilbert, S. F. 2015. 'From caveman companion to medical innovator: Genomic insights into the origin and evolution of domestic dogs.' – *Advances in Genomics and Genetics*. 5: 239–255. doi: 10.2147/AGG.S57678

Range, F. & Viranyi, Z. 2015. 'Tracking the evolutionary origins of dog-human cooperation: The "Canine Cooperation Hypothesis".' – *Frontiers in Psychology* 5: 1582. doi: 10.3389/fpsyg.2014.01582

Range, F. et al. 2015. 'Testing the myth: Tolerant dogs and aggressive wolves.' – *Proceedings of the Royal Society* B. 282: 20150220. doi: 10.1098/rspb.2015.0220

Udell, M. A. R. 2015. 'When dogs look back: Inhibition of independent problem-solving behaviour in domestic dogs (*Canis lupus familiaris*) compared with wolves (*Canis lupus*).' – *Biology Letters* 11: 20150489. doi: 10.1098/rspl.2015.0489

Wang, G. D. et al. 2013. 'The genomics of selection in dogs and the parallel evolution between dogs and humans.' – *Nature Communications* 4: 1860. doi: 10.1038/ncomms2814

Dog breeds

Asp, H. E. et al. 2015. 'Breed differences in everyday behaviour of dogs.' – *Applied Animal Behaviour Science.* doi: 10.1016/j.applanim.2015.04.010

Gim, J.-A. et al. 2015. 'Quantitative expression analysis of functional genes in four dog breeds.' – *Journal of Life Science* 25: 861–869. doi: 10.5352/JLS.2015.25.8.861

Hradecká, L. et al. 2015. 'Heritability of behavioural traits in domestic dogs: A meta-analysis.' – *Applied Animal Behaviour Science* 170: 1–13. doi: 10.1016/j.applanim.2015.06.006

Parker, H. G. et al. 2004. 'Genetic structure of the purebred domestic dog.' – *Science* 304: 1160–1164. doi: 10.1126/science.1097406

Parker, H. G. et al. 2007. 'Breed relationships facilitate fine-mapping studies: a 7.8-kb deletion cosegregates with Collie eye anomaly across multiple dog breeds.' – *Genome Research* 17: 1562–1571. doi: 10.1101/gr.6772807

Parker, H. G. & Gilbert, S. F. 2015. 'From caveman companion to medical innovator: Genomic insights into the origin and evolution of domestic dogs.' – *Advances in Genomics and Genetics.* 5: 239–255. doi: 10.2147/AGG.S57678

Smetanova, M. et al. 2015. 'From wolves to dogs, and back: Genetic composition of the Czechoslovakain Wolfdog.' – *PLoS ONE* 10: e0143807. doi: 10.1371./journal.pone.0143807

Stone, H. R. et al. 2016. 'Associations between domestic-dog morphology and behaviour scores in the dog mentality assessment.' – *PLoS ONE* 11: e0149403. doi: 10.1371/journal.pone.0149403

Tonoike, A. et al. 2015. 'Comparison of owner-reported behavioral characteristics among genetically clustered breeds of dog (*Canis familiaris*).' – *Scientific Reports* 5:17710. doi: 10.1038/srep17710

von Holdt, B. M. et al. 2010. 'Genome-wide SNP and haplotype analyses reveal a rich history underlying dog domestication.' – *Nature* 464: 898–903. doi: 10.1038./nature08837

Free-roaming dogs

Athreya, V. et al. 2014. 'A cat among the dogs: Leopard *Panthera pardus* diet in a human-dominated landscape in western Maharashtra, India.' – *Oryx*. doi: 10.1017/S0030605314000106

Davis, N. E. et al. 2015. 'Interspecific and geographic variation in the diets of sympatric carnivores: Dingoes/wild dogs and red foxes in South-Eastern Australia.' – *PLoS ONE* 10: e0120975. doi: 10.1371./journal.pone.0120975

Ericsson, G. et al. 2015. 'Moose anti-predator behaviour towards baying dogs in a wolf-free area.' – *European Journal of Wildlife Research* 61: 575–582. doi: 10.1007/s10344-015-0932-6

Garde, E. et al. 2015. 'Effects of surgical and chemical sterilization on the behavior of free-roaming male dogs in Puerto Natales, Chile.' – *Preventive Veterinary Medicine*. doi: 10.1016/j. prevetmed.2015.11.011

Ghoshal, A. et al. 2015. 'Response of the red fox to expanion of human habitation in the Trans-Himalayan mountains.' – *European Journal of Wildlife Research*. doi: 10.1007/s. 10344-015-0967-8

Izaguirre, E. R. 2013. 'A village dog is not a stray: Human–dog interactions in coastal Mexico.' Doctoral thesis, Wageningen University, Holland

Jarnemo, A. & Wikenros, C. 2014. 'Movement pattern of red deer during drive hunts in Sweden.' – *European Journal of Wildlife Research* 60:77–84. doi: 10.1007/s10344-013-0753-4

Sepúlveda, M. et al. 2015. 'Fine-scale movements of rural free-ranging dogs in conservation areas in the temperate rainforest of the coastal range of southern Chile.' – *Mammalian Biology* 80: 290–297. doi: 10.1016/j.mambio.2015.03.001

Index

Acknowledgements

THANK YOU TO Alicia, Love and Katarina who have seen me disappear into the writing bubble again for an autumn, allowing me to retell stories from the wonderful world of dog research. I'd like to thank my wife, Katarina, who has commented on my language and content. My good friend Anna Lundbäck, owner of the Dachshunds Zelda and Remus, has also contributed with corrections and positive feedback.

I also want to thank Maria Ahlberg for letting me borrow her beautiful dog Ville, an Irish Setter, for the author portraits. Anders Rådén, my versatile colleague from our time at Nationalnyckeln, took on the challenge of illustrating the book and did so with flying colours!

I want to thank my publisher, Martin Ransgart, and my editor Hanna Jacobsson, for making our collaboration so enjoyable and pleasant.